Up The "Down" Ladder

~ Simple Ideas to Overcome Depression ~

Dolores Ayotte

Up The "Down" Ladder

Copyright © 2012 by Dolores Ayotte. All rights reserved.

No part of this publication may be reproduced, stored in a retrieval system or transmitted in any way by any means, electronic, mechanical, photocopy, recording or otherwise without the prior permission of the author except as provided by Canada and United States copyright law.

Book design copyright © 2012 by Dolores Ayotte. All rights reserved.

Cover design by Dolores Ayotte

Photograph provided by BigStock Photo

Interior design by Dolores Ayotte

Printed by CreateSpace

Published in Canada

ISBN: 978-0-9948673-0-8

Self-Help, Motivational & Inspirational

Disclaimer: The suggestions provided in this inspirational book are based on a personal point of view and not in any professional capacity.

For Fred, our children, our grandchildren, and for all those who are reading my words...*with love.*

TABLE OF CONTENTS

Foreword

Introduction

1 - Little Things

2 - Personal Fulfilment

3 - Great Things

4 - The Game of Life

5 - Dare to Dream

6 - Small Differences

7 - Imagination

8 - Déjà vu

9 - The Blame Game

10 - Stone Soup

Conclusion

Bonus Chapter from *Growing Up and Liking It*

Bibliography

Endnotes

Foreword

I have always known that my mother could give sound advice if the occasion arose. I have gone to her often throughout my years at university, during my employment as a social worker, and now in my years of mothering. Sometimes as children in the process of growing up, we can't always see our mothers as women, as if the role of mother negates being a woman. I have learned to look at my mother through the eyes of a woman looking at another woman. As an adult, I see a woman who passionately cares about people, not just her own children but all people who may have suffered or who are suffering. She knows suffering, but she also knows the power of hope, knowledge, and self-love. These are such simple concepts, yet many times they are so hard to grasp in times of despair. I have had my own times of despair, from a firstborn being in the NICU to the heartbreak of some of the tougher times during the mothering of my own children. It is during those times that I have called my mother knowing I would receive the words of guidance that I so longed to hear. Her guidance is not complicated but rather straightforward and practical. Her words are just the remedy needed in times when complications and stress seem to dominate our lives.

My mother is educated, but it is more through her own painful trials that she has learned life's most valuable lessons. I feel that it is because of her compassionate heart that she writes this book full of wisdom and raw knowingness. She initially wrote her books so that her children and grandchildren could benefit from her life experience. Her goal was to spare them the suffering from falling as hard and as deep as she did during her most painful times. It is with this compassion that she shares her recipe for a more balanced life with her readers.

My mother writes in much the same way as she would talk to you if you came to her for advice. Her words are well thought out, gentle, and non-judgmental. You can feel this positive energy throughout the pages of her book. Two of the greatest gifts my mother has ever given me are: to believe in something bigger than myself, and to honor the beliefs of my neighbor. It is because of these wonderful gifts that I now see the world in color instead of black and white. What joy it has been to live life with such an open heart. Although I am her daughter, I no longer ignore the woman my mother is nor the woman my mother wants me to be. In doing so, my eyes are now wide open and able to see the gentle wisdom that was always there right in front of me. I am ever so grateful that now you too can share in my mother's wisdom and grace. In doing so may your heart be open to the gifts her book has to offer. Enjoy!

Andrea Cockerill – BA (Psychology), BSW

INTRODUCTION

I titled this book ***Up the "Down" Ladder*** because when I decided to walk/exercise, I was at a nadir or extremely low point in my life. My depression was actually so severe that I was hospitalized. In other words, I was at the bottom of the ladder when I opted to take that first step up the ladder to get out of the black waters surrounding me. I could not swim and I found myself to be in way over my head. It was a very big decision for me to learn how to help myself because at times, it seemed easier to do nothing and just go with the downward flow. The dismal draw of the murky waters can be inviting when you're feeling sorry for your personal state of affairs rather than making an effort to swim. I had this "woe is me" attitude which wasn't getting me anywhere.

In this book, each chapter will be started with a special quote that I have enjoyed. After that, *que sera, sera*…what will be, will be. I agree with John Ruskin when he says, "the highest reward for a person's toil is not what he gets for it, but what he becomes by it"[1]. The joy that I receive in the writing of this book will only be surpassed by the pleasure any of you may find in reading it. Hopefully, what I have written will enhance your life as much as it has enhanced mine. Just keep in mind that "the books which help the most are those which make you think the most."[2] This is one of my main objectives. Every word that I write is meant to be food for thought. I am merely sharing my thoughts and ideas with each and every one of you in order to spur you on in a more positive direction. I would like you to think, reflect and digest this information. After you have mentally chewed on what I have to say, spit out the parts that don't apply to you.

I'm no expert, nor am I professing to be one. I'm no different than any one of you trying to make my way in this sometimes strange world of ours. If my words help you make a better life for yourself in any way, shape or form, then I have achieved my goal of making a positive difference by lessening another person's troubles or woes. I couldn't ask for more than that! However, I do know that "the experience gathered from books, though often valuable, is but the nature of learning: whereas the experience gained from actual life is of the nature of wisdom".[3] Bring home at least in part, some of what you've read and you will attain some of your own personal goals and level of wisdom. Many times in life, we can experience "down" days. When we do, we can turn those days around if we are open to looking at some simple ways to make us feel better. ***Up The "Down" Ladder*** is meant to cheer up the reader by giving a few everyday, easy-to-accomplish examples to do just that!

1 ~ LITTLE THINGS

"It is not the straining for great things that is most effective; it is doing the little things, the common duties, a little better and better"[4]

Do you feel like you are in a rut? How many of us look at our lives and feel inadequate, insecure and unfulfilled? I'm still surprised when I hear people talk about these kinds of emotions and how alone they feel. "Instead of suppressing conflicts, specific channels could be created to make the conflict explicit, and specific methods could be set up by which the conflict is resolved."[5] In our culture, negative feelings are far more common than not. You are not unique, nor permanently scarred because you have such feelings. It's just that most people may prefer to hide what they are experiencing because they see it as a form of weakness and they don't want anyone to know or capitalize on it. At times, this may appear to be a very good strategy; however, to think that we are the only ones who struggle with negative thoughts and feelings, is only doing an injustice and disservice to ourselves. "We must become acquainted with our emotional household; we must see our feelings as they actually are. This breaks their hypnotic and damaging hold on us."[6] It is far more beneficial to embrace our negative cycles in life and admit that we could use a boost to our self-esteem.

At the beginning of this self-help book, I would like to make my point very clear. I want to stress that I am talking about what I consider to be "normal" down or negative cycles in life. You know, the times when nothing seems to be going our way and we just can't seem to do a thing right. Believe it or not, most of us have these experiences at one time or another. This is the kind of rut I asked you about in the first paragraph of this chapter. "Experience has taught me this, that we undo ourselves by impatience. Misfortunes have their life and their limits, their sickness and their health."[7] The negatives that we experience in life usually do not last forever. Life has many up and downs and learning to effectively deal with life's challenges is the only way to find the joy we are all seeking in this world we call home. If you are not happy with your life and you feel in a rut, instead of just spinning your back wheels, it is wiser to make some smaller life altering changes in order to get out of your negative situation.

First of all, we must ask and answer a few pertinent questions. For instance, is it your job that is causing you grief? Is it your home situation whether with your spouse or your children? Has it got to do with other family members or friends? What I'm suggesting here is that you have a little honest question and answer period with yourself. Perhaps, the best course of action is to merely answer these questions with a simple yes or no. I can ask you all kinds of questions to give you food for thought but I can't get inside your head to hear the answers. Only you can do that. In other words, it is necessary to do a little self-analysis. I am well aware that not all answers are as cut and dry as a yes or no but it's a start. It may help decipher the real problem areas in your life in order to help focus on the areas that require the most attention.

My daughter mentioned that the first book I wrote was far more appealing to my generation than to hers. She was right. Most of the feedback I have received is from the people of my era. They can really relate to a lot of my experiences because they've lived through many of them and quickly related to what I meant and the life lessons I learned. Ironically enough, what strikes one person as pertinent information, may be totally irrelevant to another. I find it very interesting and somewhat challenging to come up with some answers to the questions posed while trying to consider the needs of each individual. This is especially challenging when it is necessary to compose the questions in order to figure out where this younger generation might be coming from and what they would like to know. I sense that they have every desire to solve their problems but in all honesty part of the challenge for them is recognizing what the problems are so that they can better resolve them. However, I will say this. One of my observations when looking at this generation (thirty something), is their need to compare or compete. These two words are not necessarily synonymous, but at times, are confused by the parties involved. One of the questions that keeps popping into my mind and for good reason is this, "How do you reduce the feelings of comparing the workloads of each spouse and how do you reduce feeling competitive about it?" I was actually asked this particular question therefore; I am going to make every effort to answer it by distinguishing between the differences of comparing ourselves to our spouses and being competitive with them.

"We can chart our future clearly and wisely only when we know the path which has led to the present."[8] . We all know that it isn't easy to ask for advice and it's even harder to actually act on it especially when it's coming from our parents. This concept in itself is an age old mystery. Even adult children usually prefer to learn from their own mistakes or from other sources rather than learn from ours, as their parents. I think at some level, this is a subtle form of rebellion that takes well into adult life before it is recognized and eventually overcome. Embracing this concept may very well enhance the process of getting up the "down" ladder.

When figuring out how to address the question about reducing feelings of comparison and competitiveness, the initial thing that popped into my mind was the story we used to read to our children when they were young. Perhaps, you can recall it too. The title is **Goofy and His Wife**. I will get back to that story at the end of this chapter. For now, I want to address the fact that I have noticed this need to compare workloads amongst many young married couples. According to my experience, this was not a problem with my peers in our child raising years. Therefore, it is necessary to address this question from my frame of reference in order to figure out what changed. In doing so, it will provide a better understanding of how to arrive at a solution. "Life…can only be understood backwards…"[9]

In my opinion, as time unfolds and evolves, societal values may change. When I look back at my own childhood, a mother working outside the home was almost nonexistent. At least, this was the case with my own peers. Later on, as my generation became adults, it became apparent that mothers were not as satisfied with staying home because they were attaining more education and desired more equality, monetary benefits, independence, status and so on. When men were the primary bread earners, the roles were very clearly defined. As the woman's role changed these lines became smudged. Women came to realize that mothers are nowhere nearly as highly regarded as their counterparts in the work force. It would seem that this is when the battle of the wills or perhaps battle of the sexes started to set in. When you are a stay-at-home mother you may be inadvertently regarded as less than a working mother outside the home. This view may be held by some members of society including women themselves. Over the years, as women strive for more equality, this imbalance does not sit well with them. Usually, when women are in the workforce, either out of necessity or desire, they have a better sense of self-esteem or personal accomplishment because their efforts are rewarded. On the other hand, stay-at-home mothers have no reward system set up for them and therefore, at times it may seem like a thankless job.

The only way to actually reduce what I'm thinking are negative feelings, is to honestly admit exactly what you are experiencing. "There's no feeling quite like the one you get when you get to the truth: You're the captain of the ship called you. You're setting the course, the speed, and you're out there on the bridge, steering."[10] Although, a healthy competitiveness can exist between spouses, there can also be an unhealthy resentment if it is stemming from negative emotions. So let's start here. Remember for every problem there is a solution. "Each problem has hidden in it an opportunity so powerful that it literally dwarfs the problem. The greatest success stories were created by people who recognized a problem and turned it into an opportunity."[11] Okay...so what feelings are we really dealing with and where do we go from here?

In essence, you as younger wives and mothers are "in the moment". I am looking back while you are presently experiencing the types of frustration that most young mothers today can identify with...and are searching for suggestions and possible solutions for this dilemma. I think most mothers want to enjoy their young children at this stage of life instead of wishing these years away in order to experience more personal freedom and flexibility in their own lives. The main concern seems to be the imbalance in the relationship between the husband and wife and the sharing of family duties. There is a third aspect to be considered when it comes to the imbalance that may occur in a family household. At times, children can also disrupt the balance that parents might be trying to establish in the family home, by having some of their own needs and demands. I believe it is necessary to keep this in mind while I discuss the differences between comparing and competing with our spouses. I think raising a family contributes and adds to the stresses of life which may result in the need to compare. I don't sense much competition in this scenario. It is far more about comparing the workloads and experiencing frustration and anger if we think we are carrying more than our fair share of the load.

Now, I feel the need to return to the story of ***Goofy and His Wife*** in order to make some necessary points as far as comparing our lives to our spouses. I enjoyed reading this particular book because I could identify with it. I am still smiling as I remember this story so well. As far as I'm concerned this is a "must read" for all young families. It seems to capture so much wisdom in such a simple little childhood book. In this story, it is actually Goofy, the husband who isn't happy with the workload in his life. He feels that his wife is not carrying her fair share of the load and he would like this situation remedied. Due to the fact that she stays at home, Goofy doesn't see his wife as actually working as hard as he does. He may come from that old school of thought that existed in my era. The old notion of, if you're not earning money…than you are not really working.

Has this idea really evolved as much as we would like to believe? At times, I'm not so sure it has or at least, I haven't seen as much proof as I would like to see.

Now, getting back to Goofy, at his insistence, he and his wife agreed to swap roles in order to evaluate if their individual roles in the family were fair and equitable. Although, Goofy's wife went off to work and took over his job, in this book we only get to see how Goofy's life unfolded on the first day in his new job as homemaker. I was very amused as Goofy flubbed time after time in his efforts to get all the household chores done. By the time his wife returned home from work, he was so relieved to see her and eagerly wanted to go back to his old life. After this initial job switch, he had a new understanding of his wife's workload and a new found respect and appreciation for her as well. In all fairness, we never did see how Goofy's wife fared in her first day at Goofy's job. The reason for Goofy's day being the focus of this book is probably because he was the one doing the griping. At times, we can all complain about the stress we experience in life because of what we see as unfair. It doesn't only happen between spouses, it happens in the workplace over and over again. For one reason or another, this personality trait seems to have a common thread that weaves its way through many aspects of our lives.

The more we compare, the more we think we are doing and the less we think our counterparts are doing. It's this constant need to compare that ends up causing so much resentment and subsequent grief as we see our spouses coming up short in regard to our expectations of them. This is the reason I think the root of the problem is far more about comparing and dealing with feelings of resentment, rather than having a natural competitiveness that may exist in other relationships. Comparing ourselves to others in any situation including marriage has little or no positive end results. On the other hand, a healthy competitiveness can have its benefits as it encourages us to strive for higher goals and better results as we try to emulate those that we admire and respect. "There is one quality which one must possess to win, and that is definiteness of purpose, the knowledge of what one wants, and a burning desire to possess it."[12] When we reach these goals, we usually experience a better sense of self, accompanied with more confidence and self-esteem. In other words, healthy competition is good; however, comparing our workloads to others is actually negative and seldom makes us feel good. It's like using some kind of invisible measuring tool. When we see ourselves as doing more or having less than other people including our partners, it only serves to anger us and builds resentment. In most instances, these negative emotions reduce our confidence and self-esteem. In essence when we compare ourselves to others, it can have the exact opposite effect. Instead of feeling good about ourselves, we end up feeling worse. It's a no win situation.

I think the reason for so much comparison may lie in how the job of homemaker is viewed by the individual or even by society at large. Being a mother/homemaker and engaging in all the mundane tasks (wiping runny noses, changing soiled diapers, housecleaning, etc.) that go with this role in life are not necessarily highly regarded by others including ourselves. Perhaps it is necessary to give this type of work a better image, a higher job rating, more benefits, and more compensation...not necessarily in the monetary form but that wouldn't hurt either! The main way to reduce negative feelings is to realize what is causing them in the first place. My point is that it is wise to concentrate on your own role in life and your attitude about it. There is only one person that you can change in this world and that is yourself. Love what you do and everyone will want your job. The quote below makes perfect sense to me. How about you?

"Put the uncommon effort into the common task...make it large by doing it in a great way."[13]

2 ~ PERSONAL FULFILLMENT

"Great things are done by a series of small things brought together."[14]

We all know that variety is the spice of life. I've been asked what helped me gain confidence as a mother and homemaker. Initially, you may very well find my answer somewhat ambiguous but I will make every effort to be as clear as possible. To be a really good mother, you have to learn how to appreciate what you do by tapping into your creative juices. In other words, it is necessary to think outside your regular routine. Being a devoted mother and wife is an extremely demanding job. Many women gladly return to work because raising a family and being a full time homemaker can easily take up all of our energy and leave very little personal time. Full time mothers may seem like a rarity these days but they still do exist. Women that fall into this category can easily deplete their expendable energy on their husbands and children to the point where they have nothing left to give themselves. When I was at this point in my life, I couldn't see the forest for the trees. Oddly enough, I needed some time away from my children and my husband in order to better appreciate them and the rest of my life in general. I needed to feel good about something going on in my life that didn't have to do with my family. As much as I loved my role as mother, I felt that I wanted more. In other words, I desired to attain a sense of personal fulfillment and contentment apart from my family.

As strange as this may sound, it was necessary to lose myself in order to find the real me. I really think I got lost in the shuffle with the focus of being a good wife and mother on the front burner that I eventually lost sight of my true self in the process. In reality, my judgment was off and I became confused about my own goals and sense of self-accomplishment. However, here's where I went wrong when I initially re-entered the work force after being a stay-at-home mom for a few years. Perhaps you can identify with my situation and learn how to reduce the negative emotions in your life by learning from my mistakes. I returned to my teaching profession full time and continued to do everything I had previously done at home. Being a perfectionist by nature, I only succeeded in adding to my workload and responsibilities. In my perfect little world I became like super mom. I would not let anything slide on the home front with my husband, children, extended family, and friends. I just continued to do all that needed to get done. In the end, it was like burning the candle at both ends and I soon burnt out. This is when my depression started to kick in and everything in my past seem to come back to haunt me. My whole life soon fell apart. Before I knew it I was worse off than before I returned to work. I had to give up my teaching profession due to my depression and stay at home full time once again. It was necessary to re-energize and mentally re-organize how I was going to correct this mess. In other words, I had to sit in my own pew and figure things out. This was not a fun time in my life. I then had to start from square one in a new and improved way. It was a tough row to hoe because I felt like a complete failure. However, I learned one very important thing. "To fail is a natural consequence of trying. To succeed takes time and effort in the face of unfriendly odds. To think it will be any other way, no matter what you do, is to invite yourself to be hurt and to limit your enthusiasm of trying again"[15].

The next few paragraphs apply to stay-at-home mothers; therefore they may not be of interest to those of you who already work outside the home. I encourage you to read them nonetheless, as they may give you a different perspective. After this self-perceived failure of mine, I discovered that I needed to find more balance in my life in order to accomplish the sense of personal fulfillment that I not only craved but needed. Balance is a key factor in attaining all of our goals in life. Do you have balance in your life? Have you set the right goals? Through trial and error, I eventually discovered the wisdom of the following adage and the importance of setting proper goals and perseverance. "If I've got the correct goals, and if I keep pursuing them the best way I know how, everything else falls into line. If I do the right thing right, I'm going to succeed."[16] Being a good wife and mother is a wonderful thing but it can come at the expense of your own happiness if you don't feel as fulfilled in that role as you would like to be. There is nothing wrong with admitting this and it's to your advantage to do so. I would like to stress that more often than not, it is good for a mother to engage in some activity apart from her responsibilities to her husband and children. To suggest working outside the home on a part time basis when you are already physically exhausted would almost seem insulting. However, in order to achieve the satisfaction you desire in life, getting away from your regular routine may very well be the only way to do it. Please note the key words that I used in my suggestion, I said, "part-time basis". Mothers need to be around their own peer group in much the same way that children need to be around theirs. It just can't be about children twenty-four/seven. This is one of those conundrums in life where working/volunteering outside the home would actually give you energy rather than take from it if done in the correct way.

What I am suggesting is that a simple job, activity or educational course away from home for a few days a week could possibly give you more satisfaction in your home life. In the end, your children would directly benefit because you would be happier and more satisfied in your role as mother when you are home. "You will now have a starting place and a destination, and you will be able to determine what it will cost to get you there...You will be going someplace."[17] That place includes using your time as productively and as positively as possible. Remember that you can be a very good mother and still feel like an inner failure because you have sacrificed your own needs and dreams. Keep in mind; it doesn't necessarily have to be working outside the home. It could be anything that brings you the self-satisfaction you are searching for in your life. You simply must find something to do that fulfills you outside the environment that you are presently in. As I mentioned earlier, it could easily be volunteer work or some such thing. The key is to recognize that no matter how much we may love an activity whether it is work or play, no one would ever want to engage in it all their waking hours. You need to decide what you are good at and build on that for a couple of hours a day or a couple of days a week apart from your children and home responsibilities. It's about doing something just for you.

As mentioned, the previous few paragraphs may not apply to all of you. Some of you may be overburdened mothers, working full time outside the home out of sheer necessity. You do not have the option of working part-time. You might very well be overwhelmed by the responsibilities in your life that go with raising a family as well as providing an income to meet your ongoing needs. No matter how difficult it may seem, squeezing in a little "me" time is probably one of the only ways to glean a positive reward for all your hard work. As small as this reward might be, it is necessary to do something to help you better cope with your situation and find the joy in life that you so richly deserve. In the end, the activity you choose to engage in is suppose to make you feel better about yourself, not worse. Anyone can become down or depressed with his or her own life even if they appear to have the best life possible. Dare to do something different and it doesn't have to be hard. It is necessary to decide what you are good at and what would bring you the most personal satisfaction. You must learn to start small and build on something positive. Just be very cautious and try to add to your life by doing something you enjoy. It is quite easy to inadvertently add to your workload and your already frustrated state. "The indispensable first step to getting the things you want out of life is this: decide what you want."[18] No matter how good a thing is, too much of it becomes no good. That's the conundrum. Now you need to give this thought some careful consideration. What small step can you take to spice up your life?

Well...did you do it yet? Did you decide what you are going to do to achieve the peace and happiness that you crave? In other words, have you made the first step on the journey to personal peace and happiness? This journey lasts a lifetime and it's meant to be enjoyed not endured. It will take time and much effort to make any major changes in your life as we are all works in progress. After I reached the lowest point of my life, I had to teach myself how to walk all over again. When we don't feel good about ourselves we can end up in a down or depressed state which further adds to our already existing personal bad image. This is a no win situation. Therefore, are you prepared to put the time and effort needed to live your best life? I repeat...it doesn't matter what you decide to do, what matters is that you act on it. I chose to walk which I will explain in a later chapter. My choice of walking was so simple that I knew I couldn't fail at it so it was what I opted to do. I could not face another failure at this low self-esteem time in my life so I picked something that was very natural. Mary Pickford is right in saying, "what we call failure is not the falling down but the staying down"[19]. I also wanted to follow Zig Zigler's advice when he said, "make failure your teacher, not your undertaker"[20]. Walking was natural, easy, and affordable. Pick whatever you know you can do and then just do it. Action is the key word here. Energy begets energy. To get the ball rolling in the right direction, you need to act now. "Don't put off today, what you can do again tomorrow."[21] I can't stress this enough. Start today! "Success seems to be largely a matter of hanging on after others have let go."[22] Get moving now and don't look back!

Depression is a very complex thing and it has the tendency to touch most of our lives in one way or another. At times, but not always, it can be anger turned in. I have come to believe this statement to be true. I realize that it can be a challenge to work through these anger issues. However, "challenges are what makes life interesting; overcoming them is what makes life meaningful."[23] You can become very angry at yourself and what is going on in your life. You can also become angry at other people because you want to blame someone else for your depressed state or your overall unhappiness. This anger might be a result of hurt feelings and what other people have said or done to you or what they aren't doing for you. There is a natural tendency to let this anger fester inside so that it becomes so much bigger than it started off to be. Your down feelings/depression actually ends up feeding these, oftentimes, perceived hurts and resentments. Before you know it, you have a mountain to scale instead of the molehill you were facing at the beginning of your depressed state. I refer to this as the snowball effect. The ball of depression keeps getting bigger and bigger as there is a tendency to magnify what's happening to you when you are in a negative life cycle.

When we aren't enjoying our lives the way we think we should, we can become frustrated and even more resentful. We can often think it is someone outside of ourselves that is causing us to feel this negative way. Even if the harm that has been done to us is very real, it is very difficult to let go because it has been such a part of our basic being. In essence, it can be very hard to let go of this state of depression. This down mood can become like a trusted friend that you can rely on as you visit these not so positive feelings over and over again. As a result, things get into a comfortable rut. You can end up isolating yourself from other people because they may not feel as sorry for you as you do for yourself. You think that you understand yourself so much better because you know what has been done to you and what you feel inside. These inner feelings are okay for a time as you work through the healing process and try to better help yourself, but if you stay there too long, they can become your true enemy.

There is a fine line. Sitting in anger which can feed a depressed state and releasing anger are two different things. Most times, a negative emotion like anger, projected onto another person is the very thing that we do not like about ourselves. When a person is clear about what they feel and why they feel it, they can make better daily and long term decisions and not take their anger out on an innocent bystander. Lashing out in anger never gets positive results. This is quite common behavior for people with anger issues. Self-awareness is huge in healing. This concept involves sitting alone and looking within. Often times, this process can be very painful, especially if you don't like yourself. Shame and guilt can destroy a person; however, there is a place deeper in every single person that can rise above shame, guilt, and anger. This inner sanctum has the power to heal our wounded spirits. This healing power lies within every single person and it is greater than depression. This is where true hope lies.

Making the effort to get past the anger and this negative life cycle is a huge decision. It means that you have decided to let go and move on in a positive direction. It means that you have decided to forgive not only those who are adding to your grief, but to also forgive yourself. It means that you have now taken back the responsibility for the happiness in your own life. You are shimmying up to the bar and saying, "I can do this...I can get out of this funk". This decision is not for the faint of heart. "You must do the thing you think you cannot do."[24] This is a very crucial point in the healing process. It is the very first step in deciding that you want a truly happier self. It's taking back your own personal power. "Quality is never an accident. It represents the wise choice of many alternatives."[25] It's realizing that you are accepting the responsibility for the majority of happiness or unhappiness in your own life by adjusting your own attitude and choices in life. "The best thing about the future is that it comes one day at a time."[26] I want to stress once more that this is a very crucial decision. It is much more natural to feel like the victim of someone else's bad behavior toward you than it is to "grow up" and admit that your slate may not be as sparkly clean as you perceive it to be. It means you must embrace the fact that you may very well have had a hand in what is happening in your life and why you lack confidence and self-esteem.

Yuck…who really wants to look at themselves in such an analytical way? If you really want to move up that ladder, you must make a very big decision and take a very big step. This step is what I refer to as the "leap of faith" step because you are also deciding to reach out to a Higher Power and get past these not so good feelings about yourself. You are not alone. Reach down really deep, and there's a hand inside you that will reach back. Together you will find the strength, the courage, and the inspiration to move on up so you can better see the light of day! "The spirit, and the will to win, and the will to excel are the things that endure."[27] Perseverance is the key.

One of the main reasons I have decided to share my insights with you is because I have personally suffered the devastation and despair of a depressed person. I innocently let my situation get out of hand. At my lowest point, it felt like I was drowning in my own despair. I urge you to get help before you sink too low but just make sure that you get the right kind of help. At times, one can seek out counselling from a very well educated and informed person. This may work for you. "The greatest motivational act one person can do for another is to listen."[28] You might just need someone to validate what you are experiencing. I think that this option can have some great results, however it is one thing to listen and a totally different thing to give advice. For example it may be an exercise in futility to seek marriage or parental counselling from a priest or similar type of counsellor who has chosen to lead a celibate or childless life. I can't imagine any particular formal education that could give you any better credentials than the experience of raising a family yourself.

Such counsellors may very well know what they are talking about because of the formal education that they have received. However, I can earnestly say this to you, you may get a more hands on approach from somebody who has actually been through the healing process themselves and has dealt with similar issues. That's why there are so many support groups in existence today. There is no better teacher than the voice of experience. "Experience is a hard teacher because she gives the test first, the lessons afterward."[29] To get proper counselling, you must choose the right counsellor with the best credentials to suit your needs or problematic situation. It's not to say that counsellors don't know what they're talking about... it's only to say that if they have experienced or been exposed to similar situations in their own lives, they will be more understanding and compassionate. As a result, they will be better able to relate, validate, and advise you. You would then have the benefit of not only their education, but their experience as well.

I also realize that some people might need medication and a doctor's care to help relieve their depression, but I also realize that medication alone may not relieve all your symptoms. I'm sure you've all heard the expression, "the Lord helps those who help themselves"[30]. No matter the origin, there certainly is some validity to this adage. I believe where there's a will, there's a way. I also know how difficult it can be to find that way based on my own struggles. If, in anyway, I am giving you the impression that you can "snap out" of the depressed state, I apologize. This is a very unfortunate misconception that some people hold, especially those who have never experienced depression nor have been exposed to it. Just the same, in my opinion, I think a depressed person still has the capability of reaching out to others in order to help themselves. You may not be able to "snap out" of depression, but you can decide to take the fork in the road that will lead you to better mental health and healing. You can have a mental illness and still have good mental health because you are effectively dealing or coping with your illness. This situation is similar to a diabetic who has his/her disease under control by maintaining a proper diet, by exercising and/or by taking a doctor supervised medication. You can also have poor mental health without being labelled mentally ill because you merely choose to exist rather than to truly enjoy life to its fullest. Everybody needs to focus on their mental health, not just those suffering from a mental illness. This also hold true for our physical health.

    I want to stress that depression is also a very physical condition. It has been described as a chemical imbalance in the brain. As stated earlier, medication may be required to help correct this imbalance. After, I received a doctor's care I eventually made some decisions on my own in order to help myself. It was no easy feat! Depression is a form of mental illness. Over twenty-five years ago, when I found myself in this depressed state, no one was admitting to any kind of mental illness. There was and may still very well be a stigma attached to it. At that time, shame…is a good word that comes to mind to describe how I personally felt. Embarrassed by my condition…is another one that pops up. Just mortified by my experience…exhibiting anti-social behavior…and not wanting anyone to know my condition also comes to mind. Admitting and talking about any form of mental illness is no easy thing, not even today. It can be very isolating and lonely to have no one to share your thoughts and feelings with. It's no fun to be around depressed people and it is even less fun for the person who is depressed. Please bear in mind that the depressed person sits in this seat day in and day out unless they reach out and get the proper help. I agree with Ralph Waldo Emerson in saying, "the first wealth is health"[31]. Most people never fully realize how important their health is until they lose it. This makes it especially important to have good mental health because it affects your whole being.

I must admit, however, that not doing anything to help yourself will never make the depression go away. "To succeed, we must first believe that we can."[32] You really must act in order to get on the road to recovery. It's a very tough road and I will not minimize the work ahead. It is well worth all the effort if you get off "the bench" and become a worthwhile player in this sport called life. It is vital to realize the importance of reaching in for strength and also reaching out for help. You cannot do it alone. You need the strength of a Higher Power and the love, encouragement, and acceptance of those around you. I received so much strength, more than I ever thought possible, by revisiting my roots and re-establishing my faith with a loving and kinder perception of God. I learned that "God loves you because of who God is, not because of anything you did or didn't do"[33]. I cannot tell you how relieved and grateful I was to discover this. Also, try to remember that "what happens to a man is less significant than what happens within him"[34]. Within you, you can and will find your true treasure. It will help you overcome what has happened to you instead of fueling your depression.

My husband also chose to hold on to me through this unbelievably painful journey. You really do need a hand on the outside as well as the one on the inside that will help pull you through this muddled state. So first and foremost, seek help and then listen to the ones you have chosen to reach out to. In my opinion, to listen means to heed. It means heeding the advice of the people you trust and the ones God has put on your path just like my bus driver friends that you will learn more about in a later chapter. It is possible to see the light of day and enjoy life once again. Look very hard for the angels in your life. They really are there, but sometimes we can be blinded by our own pain. Wipe away those inner tears and your vision won't be so blurred. Really, someone is there for you, you just need to see clearer. It won't happen overnight. "Happiness is in the joy of achievement and the thrill of creative effort."[35] Hard work requires much effort. You may take two steps forward and then one step back, but never give up. Even when you fall back, you will have made some progress up that ladder and you won't fall to the bottom rung. Take one step at a time and keep persevering. There is no other way to get out of the black hole of depression except up that ladder to the light that you may not yet be able to see! It is there…I know because I've been where you are and I'm encouraging you to make your way toward the light.

"Life is a series of experiences, each of which makes us bigger, even though sometimes it is hard to realize this. For the world was built to develop character, and we must learn that the setbacks and griefs that we endure help us in our marching onward."[36]

3 ~ GREAT THINGS

"Do the difficult things while they are easy and do the great things while they are small. A journey of a thousand miles must begin with a single step. All difficult things have their origin in that which is easy, and great things in that which is small."[37]

After I left my teaching profession due to ill mental health, I was eventually (2 ½ years later) employed by a major financial institution. It was a big shift away from what I was used to doing. At first blush, it felt like I was starting all over again and learning totally new skills. In one breath, as far as the technical information was concerned, I had to be retrained. It wasn't long before it became apparent to me and to those around me that there was an overlap in some of the skills required by both jobs. The philosophy of the bank I was employed by was in the process of trying to change. In the past, there would be announcements made about who got promoted and who was moving up in the banking system. There was plenty of upward mobility and transferring of employees from branch to branch. It was apparent to all of us that someone higher up on the corporate ladder was making these decisions and promoting workers. Getting a promotion and a pay increase was of course, seen as a reward for a job well done. This procedure was common in most workplaces.

Suddenly, or maybe not so suddenly according to the higher ups, a program was instituted with a totally different philosophy. Management decided to involve all employees in their own advancement opportunities throughout the organization. Instead of management deciding if an employee should "get ahead", the employees had to decide what they were going to do to achieve this goal themselves. "Opportunity...Often it comes disguised in the form of misfortune, or temporary defeat."[38] At employee evaluation time, the employee actually had the opportunity to draw up a plan of how they were going to accomplish their own goals. They were asked questions like - Where do you see yourself in one, two, or five years down the road and so on? They were also asked how they were going to go about achieving this now goal-oriented plan. If they would prefer a different, higher paying position, then the employee was required to take the necessary bank courses in order to attain this personal goal. The goal of this financial institution was to lop off some of the higher paid management jobs in the typical pyramid structure that had existed for so many years.

They somehow or other wanted people to now be responsible for themselves and to make their own decisions about getting ahead.

At this time, there were many long term employees. It was not unusual, for some employees to stay in their job for years, if not for their entire working career. So what do you think their reaction was? Do you think this was well received by the employees? Do you think it was an easy transition? To my observation, it was like trying to alter the flow of raging water. It was necessary to try to re-educate the employees to actually try to think for themselves. This concept shifted the onus onto the employee as much as possible to not only be responsible but accountable for their own actions in the work force. "Success on any major scale requires you to accept responsibility…In the final analysis, the one quality that all successful people have…is the ability to take on responsibility."[39] The whole institution was being restructured from top to bottom. Efficiency experts were brought in at all levels in order to cut costs and hone the organization. What previously felt like a secure and comfortable work environment now became worrisome for a lot of employees. No one felt safe. Job security was a thing of the past. Compensation packages were being offered to those who accepted the option of leaving this organization and finding employment elsewhere. I must admit this was a chaotic time for most employees, including myself. In a lot of instances the morale was not good. Change is seldom easy and this transition period was no exception.

I was very amazed at the lack of enthusiasm on more than one front as far as this project was concerned. Several of the employees who had complained in the past about not being chosen to move up in the corporate ladder, did not embrace this new dynamic. When they were previously overlooked for promotions, they could easily put the onus on their supervisor or someone else for not getting one. With this new theme of "making things happen" for yourself, this could no longer apply. This new ideology forced people to look at themselves in a more evaluative way in order to figure out why they weren't being chosen for promotions. It also forced them to decide what they were prepared to do about it. "The lack of opportunity is ever the excuse of a weak vacillating mind. Opportunities! Every life is full of them...every newspaper article is an opportunity. Every client is an opportunity. Every sermon is an opportunity. Every business transaction is an opportunity,-an opportunity to be polite,-an opportunity to be manly,-an opportunity to be honest,-an opportunity to make friends."[40] It seemed that this bank no longer wanted any "slouches" on staff.

Previously, it seemed to be the course of action for those not getting ahead to blame the organization for not recognizing their skill and what they had to offer. When some of them got overlooked over and over again, there would be a lot of negative rumbling which in effect would have a domino, negative impact on employee morale. I can't count the number of times I would hear the expression, "the bank did this or the bank did that" by some of these complaining employees. It's as if the walls of the bank had some how employed them. To me, all of us were the bank. The people make up the bank and decide what it stands for and the kind of organization we, as a collective group, want it to be. It was very difficult for several people to look at things in this light. They needed to be re-educated to see that they could be responsible for their own plight. Ironically enough, the ones who complained the most about never getting ahead were the ones most reluctant to take charge of their own careers or job opportunities. In essence, it was quite clear to me that they wanted someone else to make all the decisions and to take care of them. To me and others like me, it appeared that "The golden opportunity is in yourself. It is not in your environment; it is not in luck or chance; it is in yourself alone"[41].

I don't want to skate around what I observed. I want to give it to you straight on. There are both leaders and followers in this world just like there are in our individual walks of life. The bank had its fair share of both, although in my opinion, the followers did outnumber the leaders. However, leaders can be born or they can be created by having the opportunity to become one. Not all leaders remain leaders for their entire lives nor do all followers remain followers. Situations and opportunities can have a huge effect on any given individual's choices. "A man sooner or later discovers that he is the master-gardener of his soul, the director of his life."[42] As far as I'm concerned there are a lot more followers in life than there are leaders but both can take responsibility for their own decisions when they accept the fact that they are the ones making them. Some people crave wearing "the hat" and want to be in charge all or most of the time. Others never want to be in charge and are not eager to the wear "the hat". There is absolutely nothing wrong with either personality type providing you respect each other and admit what you are dealing with as far as personality traits go.

As life would have it, there are those who fall into both categories. I call this the grey zone. These people have leadership abilities but they don't want to be in charge all of the time. So...now for the big question, what zone do you think you fall into? This is really where we might need to take a dose of truth serum. I know I've talked about honesty before, but honesty just like charity really needs to begin at home. Take a long hard look at yourself and your personal situation. Do you see yourself as a true leader? Do you see yourself as taking charge of the events in your life? Do you see yourself as goal oriented and having both the desire and the ability to make things happen? I could go on and on with all kinds of questions to describe leadership, but now I'll ask a few other questions instead. In most instances do you prefer to let others be responsible for organizing events in your life? Do you have a tendency to follow the crowd and go along with what the majority decides to do? Do you ever come up with some novel ideas or take charge in organizing events? If things don't go the way you had hoped for, do you see yourself as having any responsibility for the outcome?

At times, good leaders usually feel more responsible and accountable for outcomes although followers can share in this responsibility if they take their actions and work ethic as seriously as their counterparts. It is not fair to assume that all leaders are conscientious about their decisions and the impact they may have on other people's lives. However, usually they are more involved in decision making and therefore might feel they have more direct input in the success or failure of a business decision or project. Due to this fact, they may have a greater desire to make their efforts work because it is a direct reflection on whether their ideas are perceived as successful or not. On the other hand, people who are not directly involved in the decision making may not feel the same kind of personal commitment. "You always do what you want to do. This is true with every act. You may say that you had to do something, or that you were forced to, but actually, whatever you do, you do by choice. Only you have the power to choose for yourself."[43]

    I have a friend in my life that I have known since I was six years old. We started off in first grade together. This particular friend is a born leader. Ever since I can remember when it came to electing class presidents, she was the one chosen. She has incredible leadership skills and organizational qualities. This friend has held several jobs and each and every one of them has always been in management. If she doesn't start off with the position she inevitably ends up with it. If there is any one who knows how to get a job done it is her. Not all people are so lucky that their personalities are so distinctive or apparent. The opposite also holds true. Usually, true followers can be as easily identified as true leaders. However, at times, being seen as a follower doesn't necessarily endear you to others or even to yourself. Take charge people don't always understand those that need to be given large doses of direction and encouragement along the way.

When we don't address our personality type, we don't always understand why people could possibly become aggravated when we don't do things their way. As previously stated, I know that there is a grey zone when it comes to these two very different personalities and I believe I fall into this zone. There is a crossover of personality traits between the two personality types. Nothing is ever so cut and dry in life and you may very well be the same as me and find that you have attributes that can be found in both types of personalities. By having a real honest evaluation of which category we fall into, we can learn to better handle some of the changes we might want to make in our lives. Thus we can become more responsible and accountable for our own happiness. "In the last analysis, the individual person is responsible for living his own life and for 'finding himself'. If he insists in shifting his responsibility to somebody else, he fails to find out the meaning of his own existence."[44]

Once again, I would like to stress that there is absolutely nothing wrong with either personality. It all boils down to self-acceptance and mutual respect for each other. We aren't all made from the same mold. Life would be very boring if we were. Therefore, the ultimate goal is to learn to appreciate ourselves for whom we are, and to change the things about ourselves that are changeable. It is extremely difficult to alter an innate part of our basic being. We can't expect others to always do things our way either. We need all types of personalities to effectively make this world of ours go around. If you are a follower, the key is to follow the right people. Who are these people you might ask? They are the ones that we hold in the highest of regard. They stand out because of the life they have chosen to live. They are the ones that we fully respect and highly esteem because of the manner that they conduct themselves and the decisions that they make. They are the ones that we feel proud to associate with and have every desire to emulate in order to follow in their footsteps.

Followers can develop their gifts of discernment and intuition and use their gift of knowledge by guiding leaders to be all that they can be. Followers do not necessarily sit by but rather help make leaders shine and in doing so they shine as well. If you are a leader, the key is to lead, not boss, people in an admirable direction. Leaders are aware of whom they are and because of this fact they have the added responsibility to set the best example possible. It is necessary for leaders to hone their skills by seeking wisdom or counsel and reaching out to others in the spirit of humility, not superiority. The best balance between both of these personalities is based on an awareness of their need for each other in order to succeed and reach the desired goals whether they are personal or professional. If you fall somewhere in between, use your God given talents in both areas as wisely as possible. The best way to deal with all personality types is to realize, who we are, what we have to offer and to work toward achieving a common goal for the greater good. We can all achieve our goals if we learn to better work together. "There is no higher service than human service. To work for the common good is the greatest creed."[45]

"The person who renders loyal service in a humble capacity will be chosen for higher responsibilities, just as the biblical servant who multiplied the one pound given him by his master was made ruler over ten cities."[46]

4 ~ THE GAME OF LIFE

"The secret of a good memory is attention, and attention to a subject depends upon our interest in it. We rarely forget that which has made a deep impression on our minds."[47]

Do you like playing games? I'm in the process right now of playing two words games on line with some of my sisters. It's ironic how different facets of our personalities can really show up when we get into the competitive mode. It must be a very basic part of our genetic makeup to want to win. I notice that this doesn't always hold true when it comes to the game of life. When some people don't feel good about themselves they kind of "give up" at times. They may not put out all the necessary effort to make their lives the successes that they can truly be. When I was going through my own depression, I started to try many different things to draw myself out of my blue moods. Many people can become paralyzed by depression. I discovered that we don't have to do anything to be worthy of God's love, but it is in the doing that we find our self-worth. As mentioned in some of my previous writings, I started to do more reading and also engage in puzzle solving. Although, I always had an interest in solving crosswords even at a very young age, I hadn't continued to enjoy this little habit for a long period of time. When I finally found the time and desire to enjoy this pleasure once again, I discovered a puzzle called the cryptoquote I enjoyed even more. It was printed in our daily newspaper on the diversion page. It is also referred to as the cryptogram in other papers and puzzle books. By utilizing my brain and focusing on my mental health instead of my mental illness, I discovered that "there is a great treasure there behind our skull and this is true about all of us. This little treasure has great, great powers, and I would say we only have learned a very, very small part of what it can do"[48].

I know that I discussed a lot about personality types in the last chapter, but I'm going to continue discussing them in this one as well in order to get my point across. I want to continue to share with you some more pertinent, concrete examples on how I overcame much of the negativity in my own life. The following is an example of a small mental game I played with myself. Solving all these word games, gave me the impetus to have a better look at the English language. All these words, big or small, are what give us the tools to communicate with each other. "Vision...It reaches beyond the thing that is, into the conception of what can be.

Imagination gives you the picture. Vision gives you the impulse to make the picture your own."[49] As I was going through the healing process, I picked a very simple little word to describe how I was feeling. That word was "mat". I remember sharing this story with one of my sisters to better explain what I was experiencing. At the lowest point of my depression cycle, I felt like a "mat" on the floor and some how or other it felt that people were walking all over me. Some were not only hurting me by walking on me, they were actually wiping their feet on me. In other words, I had people in my life that were putting me down or adding to the negative image that I already had of myself. Stop now and think for a minute. Do you have any people in your life like this? Is there someone you see on a regular basis that makes you feel worse than you already feel? Maybe it is more than one person. Take the time to have a really good look at the people in your life. Ask yourself these questions too. Do you feel better or worse after you have been in this person's/people's company? Why is this happening? At times, people can either inadvertently or purposefully do this to another person. They may have low self-esteem themselves so they treat another person poorly to help build up their own feelings of inferiority or inadequacy. Other times, they may actually feel superior to people for whatever reason.

This is when I mentally switched the letters of "mat" to form the word "tam". To me, "tam" meant to be on top of things instead of being on the floor and feeling so negative. This is just a cute little self-help, intellectual game I played with myself as I tried to figure things out in order to help me overcome my own feelings of inferiority. I accomplished this by using mental images to help promote a more positive self-image. These "tam" personalities may actually feel superior or above others. They may have the tendency to "look down" on those around them in a kind of superior or what some may refer to as a snobby way. Although, I may have felt like a "mat" personality, I know that I never wanted to heal in such a way that I would evolve into a "tam" personality. That would be like going from one extreme to the next or like going from the pan into the fire. Both personality traits: that of feeling inferior or that of feeling superior to other people has its drawbacks. I realized then and there, that I didn't want to be either. As far as I am concerned, they are the fruit from the same tree. This is when I had another good look at that simple three letter word. I decided that I could take some creative license in using it so I opted to add an apostrophe. The new word I came up with was "am't" which is the abbreviation for the word "amount". I then made a conscious decision and a concentrated effort to try to "am't" to something in life so that I could feel better about myself. Although my personal goal was to overcome my feelings of inferiority which were fuelling my depression, I knew that I never wanted to make others feel the same way I did. I didn't want to feel better at anyone else's expense. My personal goal was to help others so that they could "am't" to something worthwhile and also develop a better self image. I wanted to develop a set of tools or skills that would work not only for me but for others just like me. I wanted to share my discoveries so that I wasn't the only one benefiting from my experiences. This has been the purpose of my book writing endeavors since the onset. My goal today is to demonstrate what I did so that you can choose to try to incorporate some of these simple little ideas into your daily living. These are very concrete examples of some of the simplest things. My daughter calls this "self-talk" and that's exactly what it is. We need to better learn to use our own mental and emotional skills in such a way that they work for us instead of against us. This takes mental discipline and exercise, but if we are persistent, we can turn our lives around. It is necessary to learn to believe in ourselves before we can achieve the desired goals. Using our imagination can help us do just that. Mind over matter is the rule I try best to follow.

Using your imagination is also a creative and rewarding way to overcome some of the adversity in your life. When you feel down and hard done by, picture yourself as a mat on the floor. You probably feel angry with those around you for not treating you properly, but instead of telling them how you really feel you draw into yourself and your own shell. Does this sound familiar or ring true to you? If so, this is when your anger may turn inward and mask itself as depression. These angry feelings can also create another problem for you. It can also have the opposite effect. It can create a rage in you and you may turn around and create a cycle of abuse, by treating other people the way you feel you have been treated. This is a no win situation. It will not make you feel good and will eventually add to your negative self image. Once again, you need to have a very honest look at yourself and make a very big decision. This is when real responsibility and accountability carry the most weight and have the most value. You must admit what you are really dealing with and what, if anything, you are prepared to do about it. Remember that the only person that you have any real power over is yourself. No one else can fix this for you. It is essential to truly embrace the fact that you must decide to help yourself. This is a kind of frightening concept because it makes us feel so responsible especially when we realize that this is where our personal power dwells and we actually have the ability to take our lives in a new direction. It means we have to rise above the blaming stage. In other words, we have to get up off the floor and do something positive with our lives. This requires work. Work requires effort. When we are down and out, what appears to be the easy way out is to do nothing. We are by human nature a habitual lot. Habits, whether good or bad, are ingrained in us. They are very hard to change. Change requires effort.

Effort = results. No effort = no results. Little effort = little results.

You get to choose just how much effort you want to make to rise above this depressed state and in the end you will achieve the corresponding results. I realize that this is a tough concept because it puts the onus on you but let's face it, it is your life. It's really is up to you to decide because no one else can do it for you. "Within you right now is the power to do things you never dreamed possible. This power becomes available to you just as soon as you change your beliefs."[50] The belief that you must work to change your personal situation is a fact that you must wrap your mind around. It is one of the first steps toward getting out of the negative cycle you might find yourself in. Taking responsibility doesn't mean to say that you will always feel happy but at least you will feel. Taking responsibility may feel messy at times, as you sort through the healing process. There is, more than likely, a need to grieve and forgive those that may have contributed to your depression. This step takes courage and determination but the end result will be well worth the effort towards healing and towards the ultimate goal of learning to love and accept yourself.

I am going to give two simple examples to show you how I personally helped correct my situation. As mentioned in Chapter 2, I had a major career change after being away from work on disability due to my depression and the aftermath that ensued. When I finally re-entered the work force, I had many new things to learn. The learning curve usually isn't an ego booster. My case was no exception. Due to the re-organization of the financial institution I was employed by, I found myself thrown into a job I new very little about. I not only had to learn the job, I was now working directly with customers. According to some organizations and businesses in the real world, there is more than one type of customer. Good customers, probably called this because of the amount of money they might have invested in the bank, are given better service. For instance, they might have a personal account manager assigned to them to ensure that all their financial needs are being met. Most account managers have offices therefore these higher rated customers are generally ushered into these offices in order to receive this personal customer treatment. They are usually offered coffee and a quiet, more private atmosphere. Have you ever noticed that some one else may be getting better customer service than you? Or maybe you are the one getting the better service and you actually already know why.

One day at a staff meeting, the manager was discussing what he considered to be the appropriate treatment of these apparently preferred or more valued customers. He suggested that they should be duly recognized and treated in a preferential manner according to their supposed customer status. As I sat at that meeting and looked around the room at my fellow staff members, I asked myself this question, "What kind of horse manure is this?" Probably every one of these people, including me, who were being asked to serve these customers in a special way, did not fall into the category of being treated that very same way. I took exception to this form of bias. I then made arrangements to talk to my own immediate supervisor and explained how I saw things. I asked him how management could request that these employees treat others in a better way than they would actually expect to be treated themselves if they were on the opposite side of the counter. I further explained that they were being asked to discriminate. I felt that every one deserved the same good customer service regardless of their ranking as a bank customer. "The golden rule for every business man is this: 'Put yourself in your customer's place'."[51] Believe it or not, at the next staff meeting this issue was addressed and clarified to my satisfaction. The main thing is that I discussed this with the person in power who could actually do something about it. I never discussed it with anyone else. I can't say that anyone else at that staff meeting even took exception to it. What mattered to me the most is that we all be treated as equals. I wanted to get my point across and I succeeded in doing so. I know that it made a difference because my supervisor acted on it and a positive result followed. See, you really can make a difference if you are prepared to stick your neck out. If you want to "am't" to something, you must be prepared to act respectfully and professionally as well as embrace the opportunity to speak up when necessary. There is no need to stand for nonsense or injustice even on such a small scale. "The choice is yours. You hold the tiller. You can steer the course you choose in the direction of where you want to be-today, tomorrow or in a distant time to come."[52]

The second example falls into the same category. This particular branch of the financial institution was rather large. As a security measure, the tellers did not have their own cash dispenser. We had to go to staff members behind what was called the cash cage or secured area with our transactions. They would dispense the cash which we would then count out to the customer.

One of my fellow employees was of East Indian descent. Over and over again, I would observe how he was bullied by one of the employees in the cash cage. The person who treated him this way seemed to be totally unaware of her behaviour, or perhaps for all I know, it was intentional. Either way, it was not an easy decision for me, but one day I decided I had a moral obligation to do something about it. I was in no position to take this employee aside and discuss the situation so I had to speak to someone else in order to live with myself and put an end to the nonsense that I was observing. I decided that the only way I could do this was to discuss my concerns with my supervisor in order to bring the situation to a head. Pretty well every person who worked in this particular area was aware of this unacceptable treatment including the supervisor I talked to about it. Everyone just looked the other way. By speaking to this supervisor, I ended up forcing her hand to actually deal with it. Perhaps, it was the impetus that she needed in order to address the problem. She acted on it immediately and spoke to the person who was bullying her fellow employee. I personally discovered that I didn't need to be a "mat" for people to walk on and I would not stand idly by and witness another human being treated in such an abusive manner. By anonymously helping this young male employee, I was able to lift him off the floor so that he could "am't" to something as well. In my opinion, he never needed to know I had a hand in the change of behavior or the events that ensued. By helping him out, it had a double positive effect, because it made me feel better about myself too. Now we were both off the floor. I realized that I could make a positive difference in others people's lives whether they were aware of it or not.

Guess what? I never witnessed that unacceptable behavior again. This woman may have had no idea how she was coming across but I will never forget the pained expression on the face of the guy being bullied. He felt so crummy but he didn't have any idea how to effectively handle the situation. However, after that day, it was over. The East Indian employee never had a clue that I went to bat on his behalf and it doesn't make one ounce of difference to me. What matters is that if you really care about people and how they are being treated, you can in most instances do more about it than you really think. We all have responsibilities and obligations to treat each other with respect. Just because we aren't the ones being disrespected, doesn't take away our personal responsibilities of ensuring that we are all being treated in a fair and equitable way. To say nothing meant that I saw this unfair treatment as acceptable. By speaking up in a discreet and respectful way, I was able to stop the mistreatment or abuse. In the end it was a win/win situation and I was better able to live with myself.

This is how you make a positive difference and gain your own self respect in the process. It doesn't have to be accomplished in a big and loud way. It can be done in such a way that all, including you, will benefit. If you really want to "am't" to something start by a few, small, altruistic acts. I can promise you that the best three letter combination of the words tam or mat is "am't". When you succeed in making even the smallest, anonymous, positive difference in someone else's life, you will be taking one of the biggest steps to making positive changes and differences in your own life. It's not always easy to walk to the beat of your own drum, but in the long run if you do it for the right reasons and in the right way, you will benefit more than you could ever imagine. Do good unto others. It's the moral and ethical way to go. I am going to repeat this famous quote one more time because I can't stress it enough. "There is no higher religion than human service. To work for the common good is the greatest creed."[53]

"I know of no great man except those who have rendered great services to the human race."[54]

5 ~ DARE TO DREAM

"The future belongs to those who believe in the beauty of their dreams"[55]

This is about a chapter of my life that is very dear to me. I was raised in a family of six children with a stay-at-home mother and a laborer for a father. Both of my parents had a big impact on my life and contributed greatly to the kind of life I have chosen to live. I am ever so grateful that my husband was raised in a similar environment. My husband and I have always been proud of our parents and our humble beginnings. This common background has been instrumental in almost every choice we have made together. In most instances, we seldom have to explain what we mean or why something matters because we just "get" each other. Most mothers in our era were full time homemakers and very few of us knew any other way. The majority of our fathers worked hard to "bring home the bacon" even if they had to work more than one job to do it.

My husband and I have discussed this often and neither of us can say whether we personally felt poor or not, but we both knew that things didn't come easy. Some people in our lives had more than we did but we were happy to have "a roof over our heads and food in our stomachs" to quote my dad. My dad would often talk about the hard times that he endured as the youngest in a family with over fifteen children. He was fourteen years old when his mom passed away and this had a huge impact on his life and subsequently ours as a family. Even at a young age, I absorbed most of what my dad had to say. Although, in my younger years, my mom was a very quiet person, what she didn't share about her background my dad did. Her family with eleven children didn't struggle quite as much as his did, but they were exposed to some hardships just the same. I would have to say that the awareness of poverty in my life as told to me by my dad had the most influence on me and in the desire to live within my means. I'm glad that my husband is of the same ilk and agrees with this philosophy. I know that this common way of thinking has been a great asset to each other and to our marriage.

I felt the need to explain our younger years in order to better explain our present day life style. Sometimes when people make a conscious effort to live a frugal life and within their own means others may describe this choice as being cheap. Over the years, I have taken my fair share of teasing over my lack of spending ways. I am known today by some of my closest friends as the coupon queen, a nickname I actually came up with to describe myself.

In my early thirties when I had my first inkling of writing a book, I was going through a period of wanting to reach out and help others. I was at the stage of my life when I was looking for more meaning to life and just wanting to make a positive difference. At that time, I didn't realize "the meaning of life cannot be told, it has to happen to a person"[56].

On reflecting back, it was at this stage, in my early thirties, when a simple little action helped me see how little things could actually make the difference I was looking for in everyday life.

One day many years ago, when I asked my twin ten year old daughters to tidy up their bedroom so that I could vacuum, they kind of put a pile of what they thought was garbage in the center of their room. When I got closer to pick up the larger pieces before I vacuumed, I noticed that there were several pennies in with the debris. When I asked my daughters why they were there, they both agreed that they were worthless because you couldn't buy much with pennies and it just wasn't worth bending down to pick them up. I guess that you can well imagine my reaction to this comment considering how I've described my upbringing and my subsequent frugal ways. Needless to say, I felt the pennies were worth picking up and you can be darn sure that I got my "two cents" worth of lecture in that particular day. I cannot believe what an eye opener this was for me and hopefully them as well. They did have some fun teasing me about this at a later date. One day not too long after this occasion, while walking up the driveway to our house, I noticed a few pennies strewn here and there at my feet. As I bent down to pick them up, I could hear my two daughters crack up with laughter from an open window in the house. They had conspired together and planted them there so they could actually giggle away as I bent down to pick them up. So much for taking my lecture seriously! We've had a lot of laughs at my expense over the years, but they have been received in the vein that they were meant to be, that of harmless teasing. "Do you know what my favorite part of the game is? The opportunity to play."[57]

I must say that this incident with my daughters is what inspired me to start what I called my "Penny Project". It got me thinking that, pennies alone really were quite worthless as far as their buying power was concerned, but it gave me the idea that everybody's pennies combined were not at all worthless. I created a small presentation with my ideas and made some transparencies for the overhead projector which I still have to this day. I tried everything to get my idea out there which was not an easy feat because it didn't seem like a big enough fundraiser to spark much interest. I presented it to all my family members and a few fellow church ladies to try to get it to take off. I sent copies of my presentation to an out of province sister as well as an aunt and uncle who lived in yet another province. I never heard much about it but I continued with my efforts nonetheless. At this time, due to my employment, I had the opportunity to take a course on effective communication. Needless to say, when it came time to make my presentation, I passionately presented my "Penny Project". I also contacted one of my pet charities with the idea in hope that we could somehow work together to use my idea as a fundraiser. I'm sorry to say that this didn't pan out.

My dad, who has since passed away, gave me some fatherly advice about this project of mine. He thought that it was such a good idea that I should somehow try to put my name to it so that I could receive credit for the idea if it ever became a success. I couldn't help but smile to myself when he said this. I told him that I didn't want any credit. I only wanted my idea to work. Well even today, after over twenty-five years, I have no idea how far that idea really went. However, I do know one thing. Every year a columnist for our local newspaper spearheads a major penny drive that she has been doing for several years now. Her project is called

"Pennies from Heaven" and that is one of the titles I suggested along with many others the day I made my presentation in that effective communications class all those years ago. Every time one of my daughters sees this fundraiser being advertised, she thinks somehow or other that I might have had an influence on its success and she phones to tell me so. I have no idea if this is true or not, but what matters to me most, is that all my daughters save up all kinds of coin and have now introduced their children to the giving of coin in a charitable way. "No one knows what he can do until he tries."[58]

Most of us have spare change hanging around. It sits idle in bottles, piggy banks, or on some ledges in our homes. I'm not the only one who knows that it can make a difference now. My children have known for years and now their children know as well. They also know something about the domino effect. You need to share your good ideas so that they can get out there for the benefit of others. By taking the time to help others, you will find that you will also help yourself in the process. It's a win, win situation. One of the transparencies that I prepared for my "Penny Project" was of a young boy throwing a penny into a wish pond. When he found it on the ground at a local shopping mall, his mother told him to leave it there because it was dirty and worthless.

He looked at her and said, "No it isn't mom…because a penny can still buy a dream" as he tossed it in a nearby wishing well. All of us would be wise to take the advice of that young boy. Big dreams start with small dreams and small ideas. If you can't do anything else with your pennies, you can still use them to buy a dream by throwing them into a wishing well. At best, it will keep them in circulation where they belong. The only reason, they have become so worthless is because we see them that way. You just might end up surprising yourself. When I had the dream of writing my first book, ***I'm Not Perfect and It's Okay***, I had no idea that it would really happen one day. Dreams do come true. Dreams are what we all must hold on to as humankind. Sometimes, it's all we have…so try to never let go.

Perhaps, our pennies can be joined in a circle of dreams similar to pennies that are attached together to make a fine bracelet which can remind us of how unlimited dreams can really be. Dare to dream!

"Today well lived makes every yesterday a dream of happiness, and every tomorrow a vision of hope."[59]

6 ~ SMALL DIFFERENCES

"Life is like a bicycle. To keep your balance you must keep moving."[60]

In life, I find that there are so many surprises. At times, we may expect to get support from a particular person and it doesn't come at all. Other times, we may think that there is no way we can count on someone else in our time of need and up pops the most unbelievable acceptance and support. Support might come from someone we may not even like or consider to be a friend. When you choose to get moving in life, especially in the right direction, you may be in for a few other surprises as well. You may discover that some individual or several for that matter whom you thought were your friends may not like the "new" you. I agree with Dale Carnegie when he says that, "the best things in life are yours, if you can appreciate yourself"[61]. When you make the big decision to turn your life around and become a "new" person, you obviously feel the need to change and will inevitably find the courage to do so. If you have been hanging around other down or depressed people and you're attempting to move past this depressed state, it could possibly become uncomfortable for them. The old adage of "misery likes company" may very well hold true here. Some people like it just where they are and prefer to sit in their own "pew" and the negative state that they find themselves in. Believe it or not, there really are some people who just like to gripe about their personal state of affairs and actually have no desire to do anything about it. "The pessimist complains about the wind. The optimist expects it to change. The leader adjusts the sails."[62]

This book is written for those of you who really want to move into the positive cycle of life. I'm not talking about the "tire kickers" out there who have no interest in really buying anything. I am talking to those of you who really are serious about making some life altering decisions. This is pretty serious stuff and I'm not going to pussy foot around and minimize the importance of what we're dealing with here. It's a very big decision to take the bull by the horns and fight for good mental health. It requires a great deal of determination and persistence. However, I do know this; a little enthusiasm for this self-help project will go a very long way and make a big difference if and when you do decide to make the effort. Any decent effort will result in some positive outcome. As stated earlier, it is only natural that effort equals results, the more the effort the better the results.

It is funny how so many of us wonder why life is the way it is, but when we look at the effort level it is not too hard to figure out why the results are what they are. If we keep doing the same thing, it is insanity to expect the results to be somehow different. When you know better, you can do better.

I am a teacher by profession although I didn't spend many years in the formal classroom. When I started my teaching career, I was only twenty years old. I remember it as if it were yesterday. I was such a kid myself considering my age and lack of experience. I actually had some concern for the students as far as my ability to teach them all that was required. We were both trying to learn at the same time. I was busy trying to keep ahead of the game. The greatest asset I had was my love for the children. "All that truly matters in the end is that you loved."[63] I was a primary school teacher and some of the methods I used were trial and error. You don't really learn all you need to know about teaching in the short courses I took at university. You actually end up learning on the job. I always remember thinking to myself even if I didn't do everything right…the one thing I could leave with the children because of the affection I had for them and they in turn had for me, was a love for school and education.

The same fact probably holds true here. I don't know everything, although my husband continually teases me when he says that I do. Everything I do know is based on my own personal experience and education. One thing I do know for sure is that I truly love people. Therefore, what I am trying to teach you here may be no different than in the way I was trying to teach those young children so many years ago. What I am basically saying, is that I am offering my ideas as an act of love. They may very well be my ideas, but by putting them out there for any or all to read, I may help someone in some small way. I don't need to know who you are, it is enough for me to know there is the possibility that you may better make your way in this uncertain world of ours. Helping others has always been my main goal. It's not about the numbers. Big or small, if I were only to reach a handful of people and have the opportunity to enhance their lives, then I have succeeded in my mission. In some way, my aspirations are similar to Helen Keller. "I long to accomplish a great and noble task, but it is my chief duty to accomplish small tasks as if they were great and noble."[64]

I want to share a cute little story with you to show how simple it is to turn your life around one step at a time. Many years ago when I was working downtown in a major mall complex, oftentimes, I would go shopping during my lunch hour. This mall consisted of many businesses, retail stores, restaurants, and pretty well everything working people might want at their fingertips. This particular day, I was having one of my "off" days. As mentioned earlier, we all have these kinds of days now and again, but this one was particularly bad. I decided I would go walking in the mall because I wasn't what one might consider to be good company in this rather foul mood of mine.

As I was walking along, I was wondering what I could do to cheer myself up and make for a better day. When I finally reached a section of the mall that had an outside door, I noticed a somewhat bedraggled man sifting through the sand in one of the big ashtrays near the door. There was no smoking allowed in this huge underground mall so anyone that came through the door had to "butt out". It was obvious to me that this poor man was searching for the longest butts in the ashtray so he could have a few good puffs. By the way he was dressed and by his actions, it was apparent to me that he could not afford his own cigarettes. This occurred almost thirty years ago before all the warnings about the hazards of smoking became so well known. Just looking at him and what he was doing made me forget all about my woes and my bad day. As I focused on him a light bulb went on in my head and I decided to do a small good deed. I went right up to him and told him to wait right where he was standing. He looked up at me and nodded his head in agreement. I turned around and went into a nearby drugstore and bought a large package of cigarettes and some matches. I quickly walked back to where the man was standing and handed him my recent purchase, receipt and all. I didn't want anyone to think he had stolen the cigarettes should he be seen with them. I suggested that he enjoy his gift and perhaps share them with some of his friends. He was very pleased, but what he said after that, changed my mood for the day and many days afterward. This was a Monday, and Mondays can be kind of blue just as it was for me that day. When this unfortunate man thanked me for the cigarettes, he quickly added, "What are you doing next Monday?" I almost laughed out loud because I found his comment so amusing. He was planning on meeting me there as often as possible, perhaps every Monday if I was willing. It was such a cute response. I couldn't help but smile at him, as I told him that this was just a spontaneous, one time occurrence and I just wanted to make his day.

In essence the exact opposite thing happened, he made mine instead. By reaching out to someone with a greater need than my own and giving in such a small way, it made me realize that it truly is better to give than to receive. I was given so much that precious day because even after all these years, it still brings a smile to my face. By doing what I did, I discovered that "no one is in charge of your happiness but you"[65].

This little story reminded me of how fortunate I really was and how by going out of my way to make a less fortunate person have a good day, it actually ended up creating a better one for me. You really cannot give away a kindness in life. The pleasure that this man had on his face was a hugely rewarding experience. He was very grateful and he thanked me for my kindness but it was me who should have been thanking him for getting me out of my own funk. He was the one being kind because he made me smile and brought so much happiness back into to my life that blue Monday. His appreciation for a simple pack of cigarettes was very obvious. He had so little that he had to scrounge through ashtrays to smoke other people's cigarette butts, yet he had so much because he knew how to be pleased with the little gift I gave him. Maybe, he had already discovered that, "life isn't tied with a bow, but it's still a gift"[66]. So you see how simply another person touched my life. This fellow never had a clue as to what I was experiencing that day. Perhaps, he was just an angel that had been put on my path. Either way you look at it, we both gained. I'm sure that I'm the one that benefited the most. I thank that fellow for taking me at my word as he waited for me to return. He had no idea what I intended to do when I asked him to stay where he was and wait. He just waited for me like I asked him to do. On that day, he had more faith in me than I did in myself. Yes, look around you and find the angels that are there no matter where you are or what you are doing. Just be open to this concept and you will see them in your midst. Just know, that "however good or bad a situation is, it will change"[67].

"Success is liking yourself, liking what you do, and liking how you do it."[68]

7 ~ IMAGINATION

"The secret of success is for a man to be ready for his opportunity when it comes."[69]

How do you find happiness in a role that can be frustrating, demanding, and physically exhausting? I'm pretty sure that you have all heard the expression of "dressing in layers". I've heard this expression used several times to describe how to dress in cold weather. When you are working out or exercising it is always best to use this strategy because as you start to work up a sweat, you can just remove a layer of clothing in order to cool down. It is so much easier to just peel off a layer of clothing as you go along rather than being caught in an overly warm outfit that you can't remove. I, personally find this strategy applicable in a lot of other situations. When I got overwhelmed in my early thirties and could not function at the same level as I once had, I had to draw from every creative resource I could come up with in order to get back in the game of life. I used pretty well every strategy and analogy I could come up with to develop my idea of getting up and getting on with life. This was no easy feat. I used my imagination as much as possible during this difficult time of my life. The stress that I was experiencing at the time was the basis for the depression that I was trying to cope with on a daily basis. After the very low point of just plain crashing and being unable to return to my teaching profession, I knew that I had to come up with a new and better plan. "If opportunity doesn't knock, build a door."[70] This is when I started to utilize more and more imagery. Remember what Ronald Reagan said about using your imagination and the fact that there are no limits to it. There are also no limits to human intelligence and wonder. Yes, you may even be in for a few surprises about yourself and all your unused talents.

To get back to my point, I decided to view my life as a kind of work out. This is how I pictured myself. When I felt so stressed out, my coat was so heavy and burdensome. It was such a load on my back that I seemed to be wearing all year long therefore I decided to look at my life in layers. As I began to get stronger after first falling down to put it mildly, I decided to keep my life as simple as possible. I felt like a miserable failure and I sure as heck did not want to fail to that extent ever again. So, I started very simply after my first major crash and engaged in tasks I knew I wouldn't fail at like some of the ideas I already mentioned. "Motivation is what gets you started, habit is what keeps you going."[71] I adjusted several other things in my life as well. Instead of working outside the home full time, I settled for less income and more peace of mind and time with my then younger children. You might say, "Well you could afford to do that and not everyone can". Financially, it may have appeared that I was able to do this a little more than someone else, but this wasn't necessarily the case. I could use the income just as much as anyone else, but emotionally, I could not afford to do otherwise.

In order to be truly productive and feel fulfilled, I had to mentally agree to settle for what appeared to be less and in the end I received more. I ended up with a lesser job, with less income, but with more contentment and general satisfaction than I ever had before. By working fewer hours, I had time to start my walking exercise program, to take courses, to get my housework done, to cook homemade suppers, to go to my children's school activities, to volunteer at the school library, to teach Christian instruction, to visit my parents and my not so well mother-in-law and on and on. "The successful man will profit from his mistakes and try again in a different way."[72] Now that I saw my life in all these manageable layers, I learned to truly realize the meaning of the cliché "less is more" because that's exactly what I ended up with.

When I felt a little too overwhelmed in all that was going on, I removed a layer. I didn't need to do everything. I could do what I chose to do in most instances. In other words, I better mentally organized my life so I felt more in control of it. I decided that I was in the driver's seat and I was driving this vehicle of mine. I was driving the car... the car was no longer driving me! Big decision! I agree with Henry Ford when he says that, "Failure is the opportunity to begin again more intelligently."[73] Over and over again I needed to access and re-access what was going on in my life. I became a pretty deep thinker as I evaluated what was really important to me. Some things were far more important than others. Some things were more dispensable as well. Some things I enjoyed doing more than others, but they may not have been as high a priority as other duties or obligations on my "to do" list. We all have tasks in life that we just as soon put off doing or not do at all, but we must do them in order to feel better about our lot in life. In most instances, I always do the chores I like to do the least, first. In other words, I fulfill my necessary and not always the most enjoyable obligations first. The longer I procrastinated about doing the things I didn't like to do, the more burdensome they became. The sooner I got these tasks out of the way, the better I felt and the more control I wielded over being responsible for my own happiness. "We are built to conquer environment, solve problems, achieve goals, and we find no real satisfaction or happiness in life without obstacles to conquer and goals to achieve."[74]

I want to use another analogy here to make my point. Mental visual images often clarify what words have difficulty expressing. Many times over the years as we share meals with our adult children, I have observed the many different and unique personalities that exist within my own family just by noticing the way they eat. At times, in jest, we have even discussed this with them at some of these meals. I want you to just take a little look at yourself and your own eating habits as I ask you a few questions to make my point. When you put food on your plate, can the different foods touch each other? Do you only take helpings of what you like to eat or do you take a little bit of everything to make sure that you have a well balanced diet? When you eat your plate of food, do you eat the food you like best first or last? You probably think I'm being pretty anal right about now, but I'm serious. Finicky or picky eaters may need the "I's" dotted and the "T's" crossed in other areas of their life as well. People who don't like different foods touching on their plate may be picky or perfectionists in unrelated situations. All of these points may be of interest when it comes to personal eating habits, but the one that grabs my attention the most is whether you eat what you like most, first or last. Some people eat everything they should eat first (like their salad and veggies) and then sit back and savor what they really enjoy eating at the end of the meal. Others quickly gobble up their favorite food first and then hope they have no room left to eat what they know they should eat. So, I'm asking you to just look at what you do when eating a meal to get a better grasp of a small picture of your personality type. Overall, one of the things I'm suggesting is to have a better look at yourself in order to get a clearer picture of your personality so you can may a few simple changes if need be. Start by learning to change something as simple as your eating habits. After that, see if you can develop the desire to change some of your other habits that may have a much greater impact on your personal well being. In life, if we take the time to look at some of our simple daily activities, we can get a greater understanding of our personality type and what really makes us tick. It is necessary to get to know ourselves in an honest and truthful way in order to make any changes in our circumstances. "Each time you are honest and conduct yourself with honesty, a success force will drive you toward greater success. Each time you lie, even with a little white lie, there are strong forces pushing you toward failure."[75] It is not an easy task to be truthful even to oneself! I know that you may find this hard to believe, but we can actually suppress how we really feel and bury it deep within ourselves. At times, we may even need counselling to get to the bottom of the truth because it is so painful for us to own up to it. The truth can be hidden in our past which now affects how we behave today and how we deal with people and present day events. In order to move forward and to make some necessary changes in a positive direction, we may have to face or walk through some not so pleasant memories. This is what I mean about being really honest with ourselves. We actually can live a lie and not even know it until we do some soul-searching. We are creatures of habit and most of us do not want to rock the boat.

Here, I'll give you another example. Do you ever notice just how habitual we all are and how predictable we can become? Do you go to church on Sunday or do you attend any kind of classes and try sit in the same place every time? I am presently taking line dancing classes to get some much needed exercise as well as a little socialization in with my peers. I am relatively new to this class and it is actually much too advanced for my level of skill. I want to attend because I not only need the exercise but I really enjoy the people. This is the only class available throughout the summer months. Therefore, I attend these advanced classes for the social aspect regardless of my lack of proficiency in this domain. When I first started to attend this class, a lady sitting by my side before the class started cautioned me to wait until the regulars took their places before I took mine. She added that everyone had their spot. Does that sound familiar to you? Isn't it comfortable to always go where we've been before because it's so familiar to us? Think about it and then just have a good look at yourself. "The chains of habit are too weak to be felt until they are too strong to be broken."[76] I know that we are such a habitual lot and most of us merely want to stay within our comfort zone. Now every time I go to line dancing, I stand in the spot I found for myself because I don't want to hone in on someone else's space. The same phenomenon occurs at other group activities. People mostly want to stick within their own comfort zones of sitting or standing in their usual spot. They, generally speaking, also want to sit and eat with the same people as well. This also applies to socializing with others. It is quite difficult as you age to truly embrace new people because it requires so much more effort than just socializing with our usual circle of friends. "The beginning of a habit is like an invisible thread, but every time we repeat the act we strengthen the strand, add to it another filament, until it becomes a great cable and binds us irrevocably thought and act."[77]

By taking a long hard look at ourselves in just this simple little way, it gives us food for thought as far as our own habitual behaviour is concerned. It also opens our eyes to the predictability of our own behavior patterns. "The more deeply the path is etched, the more it is used, and the more it is used, the more deeply it is etched."[78] I'm pretty sure that we all want to see ourselves as these broadminded flexible individuals, but in most instances I beg to differ with this evaluation. We, as human beings, can be very resistant to change. Even if what is going on in our lives, just plain sucks, we know what to expect and in a lot of instances we will just settle for it rather than change our actions and face the unknown. We crave security and usually want to know where we stand. Therefore, in other words, we may not like our personal state of affairs, but in reality we might not have the greatest desire to do anything but complain about our circumstances.

I know that, at times, I can be quite frustrating when I become repetitive, but for every problem there is a solution. When and if I feel the need to repeat myself I ask you to bear with me. Some points need to be stressed more than others. I see myself as a problem solver. If someone comes to me over and over again with the same problem, I innately want to help them fix it. Not all people operate this way. Some people only want to talk about their problems with any and every one who will lend them an ear. Are you one of those people? Do you only want to talk about your problems and not solve them? Be honest with yourself! "You can't make wrong work."[79] If you are and you realize this about yourself, then at least you are one step closer to doing a reality check. You may very well, like to talk and share your perceived negative plight with others but in fact, have absolutely no desire to make a single change in your life. That's perfectly fine. It's your choice. No one else may even be asking or expecting you to change. However, if you really want to help yourself then it is necessary to decide that you are going to have to make some changes to get where you want to be. "Though our character is formed by circumstance, our own desires can do much more to shape those circumstances; and what is really inspiring and ennobling in the doctrine of free will is the conviction that we have real power over the formation of our own character."[80]

For example, if you would like a better, higher paying job, you may have to better educate yourself in order to pursue this dream. If you would like to be in better physical condition, you may have to alter your eating habits and enrol in an exercise class. If you feel that you aren't getting along with people in the way that you would like, you just might have to take some courses on human relationships or spend some time reading the applicable books. Most good fortune that people experience has absolutely nothing to do with chance. People who are successful have almost always contributed to their own success by their own efforts. People with self-discipline and goal oriented lives usually achieve their goals because they are focused and determined to do so. In most cases, success is far more about hard work than any kind of luck. Most of us have to create our own luck! Why would it be any different for you? If you want to be successful, than it is necessary to, not only be responsible but accountable for your own actions or lack of actions. The key is to "do a little more each day than you think you can possible do."[81]

To me, life is kind of similar to an elastic band. The more you stretch yourself out of your comfort zone, the more comfortable you will be in it. As a result, the more comfortable you get in this new expanded zone, the easier it gets. To better use my analogy, the elastic eventually loosens up and more easily stretches to accommodate the "new" you. "Great men are little men expanded; great lives are ordinary lives intensified."[82] The goal is to make sure you take your time to increase your comfort zone in such a way that the elastic band doesn't snap. It is necessary to learn how to continually grow within the comforts of your own desire to better change your personal situation. Change is never easy! For every action, there is a reaction. Even one small change in your life, will create a change in the lives of one or more people who are close to you. As positive as the change in your behavior may be, there might very well be others around you, that will have difficulty adjusting to the "new" you. They might not want to join you in your new or expanded comfort zone. Although, you are ready for a change, it doesn't necessarily mean to say that everyone or anyone else in your sphere of influence wants the same as you. Life…there is never a dull moment. It takes plenty of courage to make changes in your life even if they are for the better. Remember to look for support in unexpected places and from unexpected people.

"Work joyfully and peacefully, knowing that right thoughts and right efforts will inevitably bring about right results."[83]

8 ~ DEJA VU

"Writers aren't exactly people...they're whole lot of people trying to be one person."[84]

That would be me! I am one such person and I have a sneaking suspicion that all authors are as well.

Are you an avid reader? Have you ever noticed that the more you read the more familiar a book can be to you even if you have not read the book before? I have found that as the years go by, it seems some how or other I think I have either seen or read something that would have been virtually impossible for me to have done so. Sometimes it's a brand new book, or the first television show of the season. On such occasions, I know that I couldn't have been exposed to either of these because they are new releases yet there is this nagging familiar feeling when I actually read a new book or watch the airing of a new show. This is when my husband and his teasing ways start to kick in. He continually tells anyone who will listen to him that I have seen pretty well everything at an earlier date. I must admit that he is finding this a lot more amusing than I am as I have been at the brunt of his many jokes. Hey…I must admit that I really don't mind because it helps keep me sharp. I have made every effort to match his wit. It actually keeps me on my toes because some comments really do come right out of left field! There must be someone else out there that shares this talent with me.

I think that the quote at the top of the page pretty well sums up what I'm trying to put into words. The more of life that we are all exposed to whether by reading, observing, or just plain living, the more we accumulate in our minds. We save all this information somewhere in the recesses of our memory banks. "There is no such thing in anyone's life as an unimportant day."[85] If you happen to become a writer at a later stage in life much like me, you need to draw from this information. There is no way that I would be able to write a book without this wealth of knowledge at my fingertips. This knowledge is stored inside my memory bank for me to draw from whenever the need arises. Most of us have a memory bank full to the brim with all kinds of material we could write or talk about. If we choose to do so, all we need to do is take the time or have the desire to tap into this resource. "Life is like a cash register in that every account, every thought, every deed, like every sale, is registered and recorded."[86] The mind, and all the information it can hold is absolutely wonderful. Its capacity is so great. The full use of it is yet to be realized. I just love what our mind is capable of and all the information it can store. It is beneficial to not underestimate the power that lies within us. Just like Bishop Sheen said in the previous quote. Everything is there. Just imagine, after years and years of living, what is recorded inside all of us. This is the reason I agree with William James as well when he states that, "the greatest use of life is to spend it for something that will outlast it"[87]. What better way to do this than to write books?

As I continue to get into the "meat and potatoes" of this book, I wanted to explain my view on how important it is to educate ourselves and store the information that we will eventually require down the road in order to better enhance life. Everyday is so unique in the sense that if we open our minds to learning something new, we can do so on a daily basis. "We are continually faced by great opportunities brilliantly disguised as insoluble problems."[88] If we take the time to think things through and analyze what is going on, more than likely we have access to the solution based on what we have been exposed to over the years. My husband always says that for every problem there is a solution and from my point of view, life certainly has its fair share of problems. Therefore, once again I feel the need to stress that this book is being written to give some examples of the solutions I have used over the years to help me overcome some of these problems. "Constant and determined effort breaks down all resistance and sweeps away all obstacles."[89]

I also like to refer to events that are happening in the present or to draw from my own memory bank in much the same way I am encouraging you to do. People can find many different alternate ways to help themselves better cope with life. We all have our unique talents and it is up to the individual to try to find the ones that best meet their own creative abilities. Although, I have found a few ways to help me, the one that I first chose happened many years ago during my first encounter with depression. After work one day, while I was sitting on the bench at a busy intersection waiting for the bus to come along, I had a brain wave. I was just sitting there in a funk feeling sorry for myself in my depressed state and I proceeded to give myself a real talking to. I concur with Thomas Paine when saying, "the harder the conflict, the more glorious the triumph"[90]. I just decided to look at myself and my situation. I opted to figure out what I could do about it. I didn't feel like facing another failure in life, so I tried to come up with a least one thing that I knew I could be good at. Guess what it was? I decided to get my butt off that bench and start walking. I knew I could at least do that right. It was a lovely spring day and the sun was shining brightly, so there couldn't be a better time to put this plan into action. I didn't need any special supplies or any kind of gear with the exception of good footwear, so off I went. Right then and there, I just got off my butt. I merely walked along the same route as the bus line and when I got tired, I just hopped on the bus when it came along. As I walked I started to hum the song "These boots are made for walking and that just what they'll do"[91]. Any time my depression tried to creep back into my mind, I just put my foot down and let my boots walk all over it. It really felt that it was time for me to wise up and do something more constructive with my life. "Wisdom is not a product of schooling, but of the life-long attempt to acquire."[92] Yup...enough was enough, I needed to shape up!

I can't tell you just how much I've walked over the years because I started that day and I have been walking ever since. My goal was to super navigate the globe mile wise by just walking on my own turf. The bus driver on my route got to know me so well that he watched as I got farther each day. He got to be such a trusted friend. As the days went by he would wait for me as I was crossing a major intercession so I could get on the bus for the rest of the ride home. Before you know it, we were smiling back at each other as I got in better condition. I was only thirty-five years old at the time. That very special bus driver helped monitor my progress, as I eventually would wave him on, because my distance increased to correspond to my better physical condition. I lived six miles from my place of employment. I started off this regime by just seeing how far I could walk until the bus came. After doing all this walking for days on end and as my stamina increased, I walked farther and farther until I walked the whole six miles home. That bus driver was such an inspiration to me, as he waved to me day after day and encouraged me along the way. "Kind words can be short and easy to speak, but their echoes are truly endless."[93] An angel had been put on my path and I am forever grateful. Look for the angels in your life. They are all around you, you just need to reach out and touch them. They have been put there for a reason. It is necessary for each of us to learn to trust in their guidance and support.

    I must have a penchant for bus drivers because initially when I boarded the bus, another bus driver would talk to me on his way home from work after his shift. He too, would watch my walking progress and monitor my increased endurance. He decided that he could also use some exercise and he asked my permission to join me in my walks when they coincided with his shift. I told him, "no problem" as long as it was okay with his wife. My husband was fully aware of my bus driver friends, but I wanted to make sure that I wasn't causing grief to anyone else's spouse. I wanted to stick to my motto of "not building my happiness on the unhappiness of someone else". He checked with his wife and sure enough, she was fine with it, so now I had a walking partner on some days. This really helped me stick to my regiment. I even walked in the winter, but not the whole distance as our winters are so severe. I can say this though, "these boots were made for walking and that's just what they'll do"[94], because twenty-five years later, I'm still up and at it. I can't help but wonder how many miles I have actually walked.

So now you know what you need to do. Pick something easy that you know you can do. Pick something that doesn't require any special training and that doesn't involve any type of competition at least at this point in your life. Pick something that is free or close to it so that it's affordable to you and then just do it! Get off your butt just like I did and you might be very surprised how a little positive action can work. Feeling sorry for myself never got me anywhere. Doing something about it did. Get a move on now. "No matter how you feel, get up, dress up and show up."[95] There will never be a better time. You know what else? You will meet some neat people and make some pretty special friends along the way. You can't ask for more than that. There are angels everywhere just waiting to help you out. Realizing this and taking the first step to reach out, is the first step on that bottom rung to *Up the "Down" Ladder*. "The future depends on what we do in the present."[96]

As I end this chapter, it makes me recall so dearly that sober time in my life when I allowed myself to trust people again. Those two bus drivers enhanced my life in such a memorable way. I am sure they have no idea the impact that they had on me at this low point of my life. The one who walked with me, of course, knew me by name. The one that drove the bus and encouraged me along the way never did. However, he will be forever appreciated for reaching out to me in my time of need in such a way that I'm sure he never even realized. His actions have etched a special place in my heart and unbeknownst to him, I will be forever grateful. "The value of a man resides in what he gives and not in what he is able to receive."[97] These were two such honorable men. Angels…yes, they are all around us! I can assure you that if you just open your eyes a little wider, you will see better. But please remember that how you view the world is what you reflect to those around you. Remember to give your attitude a tweak to get the full benefit of my recommendations. "Kindness is the noblest weapon to conquer with."[98]

Oprah's right when she says that "the happiness you feel is in direct proportion to the love you give"[99]. Genuine love shows…it is like a camel in the desert. It's impossible not to see it as you look across the barren horizon.

"In dreams and in love there are no impossibilities"[100].

9 ~ THE BLAME GAME

"Continuous effort is the key to unlocking our potential"[101]

Do you ever play the blame game? This has to be one of the most destructive choices when dealing with depression. It is so tempting to blame someone else for your personal state of affairs. I fully realize and acknowledge that people hurt each other. I'm not taking away from the sorrow that many of us endure by what may have occurred in each of our lives. Yes…we may have every reason to be depressed. However, to sit in the depressed state without making any effort to rise above it, will allow what happened to you in the past to continue to live forever and be a huge black cloud over all that you do. Shit happens! I'm sure you know exactly what I mean. There is no disputing this point. The point I am trying to make here is that you can allow it to happen over and over again by not letting go of past hurts and grievances. The questions that begs to be answered, is why would you allow someone to not only destroy your past happiness, but to have such a huge impact on your present or future happiness? Although, it has been said that there is a genetic predisposition to depression, I also know that it can either be fed or starved. To dwell on the bad things that happened to you in the past is the wrong path to follow. One of my sisters frequently uses the quote "let go...let God". This is an excellent rule of thumb to follow. You will never heal and overcome your depression if you are not prepared to let go of past hurts. It is a very comfortable state to wallow in self-pity but I can assure you that it is not the best route to go. If you are the type of person that really wants to "get even", then you know what you need to do? You need to "get well". I did it and so can you. I'm not saying it is going to be easy; however, it is well worth the effort! Forgiveness is a direct route to living your highest potential.

I've noticed something else in my travels. At times, the recollection of what happened to us to cause our depression can be skewed. It can build up in our minds as being much worse than what really occurred. It is only human to want to "pay back" others for what we think they did and for the grief that they caused. If someone was really mean spirited toward you and caused you nothing but grief, I repeat, the best way to "get even" is to "get better". Remove your invisible "kick me" sign and don't allow anyone to get the better of you. Stop... and I do mean stop allowing people to put you down. It seems to be a human flaw that if someone feels lousy, someone else will capitalize on it. I hope that you read me loud and clear on this matter because I can't stress it enough. Work everyday at building up your self-esteem and your self-confidence. Make this the basis of your "new you" structure. Picture this concept in your mind as you strive to overcome the negative feelings and negative cycle that you are experiencing. "There are no great limits to growth because there are no limits of human intelligence, imagination, and wonder."[102] You may very well have every reason to be angry at the way you were treated in the past but to let it get the best of you will never help you correct your present situation. Get up…get moving…do something…anything to get your life moving in the right direction. This is what you need to do the most. Remember that depression is often described as anger turned inward. You may very well be angry at someone who has inadvertently caused your depression and they may not be even aware of it. I'm going to repeat myself one more time. In order to truly heal you must be prepared to let go. To continue to dwell on the past only gives it more power to fuel the negative consequences of the depressed state. So in other words, be prepared to stop playing the "blame game". Follow Regina Brett's advice. "Forgive everyone everything."[103] Forgiving another person who has hurt you can be very difficult, so we need to practise forgiveness. Start small, offer forgiveness for little things that occur in your life (i.e. a person cutting you off in traffic, a grouchy spouse, etc) and build it up to forgiving the larger hurts, and then ultimately to forgiving yourself. It has been said that, our inability to forgive ourselves, is the source of most of our unforgiving feelings towards others.

Okay, so now we've agreed to embrace our past without denying what took place and how it made us feel. We're also agreeing to look at our present situation and learning to live one day at a time. Each and every day, we must strive to come up with at least one good thing that we are grateful for in our daily lives. This good thing can be as simple as the fact that today you are not pushing up daisies or that you are on the right side of the sod. You are alive and breathing. Isn't that a good thing? Then thank God for your life. Is it sunny outside? Well there you go. Thank God for the beautiful weather. Is it raining out side? Well there you go, thank God for cleaning up the dust around you. Is it cold outside? Then, thank God for putting a roof over your head or for providing some warm blankets to swaddle yourself in. Is there clean water running out of your taps? Well isn't that something to be grateful for? How many people don't have such a luxury? Is there food in your fridge and in your pantry? I know I could go on and on, but you get my point.

Open your eyes and thank God for all these little things in your life. Everyday, be grateful for your life and the simple pleasures in it and I can guarantee you that things will start to look up. Once the days start to improve, the future will also start to look brighter. After awhile, instead of looking back in sadness you will eventually learn to look forward in happy anticipation. Look it, I'm no rocket scientist. I'm one of you. This is just common sense stuff that I'm taking the time to write down. Try my ideas. I know they work! These are pretty simple, inexpensive suggestions. It won't cost you a dime to try to put some of them into practice. Go ahead…try and prove me wrong. Over time you will begin to realize that "life isn't fair, but it is still good"[104]. Go for it. You have nothing to lose! At times, we will let a perceived negative moment color our whole day. When we start complaining about "how terrible life is", it would be a good idea to, perhaps, ask ourselves to recall a few positive things that happened that day. These positive recollections may counteract the negative one that we want to complain about. Hopefully this will teach us more perspective.

My mother used to make me laugh. Sometimes when my dad wasn't behaving in the manner she wanted, she would eventually get frustrated and give him a good talking to. After that, he would pull up his socks. He would eventually come around and apologize for his unacceptable behavior. My mother would tell me later that all he needed was a little "pep talk" to get him out of the rut he was in. I use this very same technique with myself and my own family. Every now and then we could all use a little "pep talk". This is exactly what I'm trying to do in this book. We don't always have that someone who is ready, willing and able to give us the little "pep talk" that we require. Therefore, I'm in the process of trying to give all my readers a boost in life to help them overcome what's ailing them. By doing so, I'm also in the process of helping myself. I give myself these talks all the time. If I'm not talking, I'm thinking or I'm writing. Writing has become a very creative outlet for venting my own frustrations. It has been an unexpected therapeutic consequence of reaching out to help others. So you see that therapy doesn't have to have a big price tag. Writing is a pretty cheap and beneficial hobby. Reading is also of great benefit and not too costly either. There are many affordable ways to help you overcome whatever is causing your depression. One thing I know for sure is that you can't afford to stand still and do nothing. The price tag is much too great. "Make peace with the past, so that it won't screw up the present."[105]

It's kind of neat that I have chosen to write this chapter at this time. Now that my husband and I are retired I find that they're are many hours that must be filled each day. We want to be productive with no longer having the obligations of a regular job. Sometimes my husband will look at me and ask what we are going to do for the day. At times, I don't have a clue how to keep our lives both busy and exciting. I really have to put on my thinking cap because I know that we still have plenty to offer, it's just finding a creative outlet for our particular assets. "No matter what the level of your ability, you have more potential than you can ever develop in a lifetime."[106] After I wrote my first book, a couple of my friends asked me what I would come up with next. Wait until they hear our latest adventure. When I told one of my daughters just last night, those were her exact words. "What next!" I'm not so sure that she meant it as a compliment. Well guess "what next" is?

They are filming a movie in the city where we live, and my husband and I are filling in as cast extras. He's actually there today, while I'm at home. It's a good thing for him to get out of the house and amuse himself. Perhaps, I should admit that he actually does these things to amuse me.

Neither of us has ever done such a thing before and it has been quite the learning experience. It is one slow process as the director films one take over and over again. As an extra, I can never figure out what was wrong with the first take. These film makers must have money to blow because on my nickel we would have been out of there pronto. I must admit, it was kind of like watching paint dry. It was both interesting as well as long and drawn out at the same time. It was suppose to be a minimum of eight hours and it ended up being a thirteen hour day. By the end of it all, the extras almost fell asleep in their chairs; however, when the director finally decided he didn't need us any more, I never saw people move so fast. I couldn't help but laugh when someone in charge shared with us that the thirteen hours we spent filming consisted of a page and a half of the screen play. I can't even begin to imagine what it is like to make a really big movie. So my point is, there really is always something to do to get you out of your rut in life. Just give yourself a little "pep talk" and then go find it. "Your range of available choices…right now…is limitless."[107] My husband is probably cursing me right now, especially if this ends up being another thirteen hour day. Although you never know, some talent scout might spot him and give him a few words to say. If this were to happen, I'll be forced to ask him for his autograph. That would really make his day and he might see the full benefit of my creative ideas.

I have a sneaking suspicion that my husband won't be asking me what we are going to do for awhile because he has no idea what I will come up with next. This old dog still has a few surprises in her and I'm not about to dole them out all at once. Often times, I have thought that it's a darn good thing I'm not in charge of anyone because I would probably put everyone to work. You have no idea how many times I see idle people who want to get paid for doing pretty well nothing. It's a good thing they aren't asking me what to do next. I'm sure if I put my thinking cap on, I could come up with several suggestions. Aren't you glad that you are only reading my book? You don't have to actually do a thing I recommend. However, I feel the need to add this comment. It would probably do you a lot more good than harm if you did. So you see, you are also getting a little "pep talk" in order to get you off your butt and headed in the right direction. Be creative and be open to a variety of ideas. "The one thing over which you have absolute control is your own thoughts. It is this that puts you in a position to control your own destiny."[108]

To sit around doing nothing but feeling sorry for yourself and your plight in life is the most unproductive and unrewarding choice you could possibly make. Just look around you. There is plenty for you to do as well. Start small. Figure out a way to get out of the rut you are in. "You need only to choose…then keep choosing as many times as necessary. That is all you need to do. And it is certainly something you can do. Then as you continue to choose, everything is yours…"[109] It's not a matter of being anyone's fault. It's not about blame. It's about rising above your lot in life and finding something good in it. It's about appreciating the small things and using a better attitude to create more of them. Feeling sorry for ourselves and blaming others is similar to spinning our back tires in the mud. It is very necessary to look at the situation with a clear head. By doing so, fresh ideas will unfold in order to help you figure out how to fix the mess you're in. You are the only one that can really decide to help yourself. No one else can do it for you no matter how much they may want to help. It really is up to you! You may very well have a big job ahead of you but life is never without its challenges.

"Big jobs usually go to the men who prove their ability to outgrow small ones."[110]

10 ~ STONE SOUP

"Leadership is based on inspiration, not domination; on cooperation, not intimidation."[111]

Have you ever considered your self to be an underdog? Although I have internally referred to myself as an underdog when it comes to life, I'm not quite certain I know exactly what this expression means. Instead of going into a big diatribe about what I think it means, I just want to use it in the sense that actually applies to me and the life I have led. I've already described to you as far as my background is concerned that I had poor and simple roots. Like many of their peers, my parents were not well educated nor did they command large incomes. I don't want to say that I was born on the wrong side of the tracks, but I'm sure there were some people who thought that's exactly where I lived in my youth. I remember the mother of my closest friend telling her she didn't want her to play with me. You know what little children are like, they repeat things verbatim. My little friend didn't hesitate to share this information with me when I asked her to do something with me. I came from a family of six children and we didn't live in the most desirable neighborhood. Next door to us, there was a single mother with nine children living on welfare. There were other kids in the area who were always up to some kind of mischief. Some of the boys would get into some pretty serious trouble and a few of them ended up in a reform school for juvenile delinquents. Mind you, by today's standards with all that is going on with drugs and gangs etc., what these boys were up to was probably what the police would now consider small potatoes. My dad was pretty strict with us as children but there was no way that he could have prevented any of us from seeing and knowing what was going on in the neighbourhood. I was sixteen years old when we moved to a more upscale area of the city. By that time, I had already developed what I consider to be my "street smarts".

The one thing I remember when I was young, is that I never looked down on anybody. Maybe it was because even as a child there were actually some people looking down on me. I instinctively never wanted to make another person feel the same way I did when this happened. There wasn't one person I would consider to be less than me or not good enough to be my friend. In retrospect, I now know that I was being looked down upon especially when I recall some of my childhood experiences. However, as I go down memory lane and revisit that very house I grew up in, it no longer holds the negative stigma it did when I was young girl. The street is much improved with some houses being replaced by much nicer ones. It actually looks quite lovely now. I think one of the best things about being a child is having the innocence to see things in such a lily white way that we think everyone views the world the same way we do. It's only after you experience the full gamut of life, that you may allow ourselves to become more jaded. It doesn't necessarily have to be this way. I think we allow ourselves, with emphasis on the word allow, to become jaded. In order to better enjoy our lives, we must make every effort to get past our negative life experiences and relearn to look at life from some of our innocent childlike perspective. It's a pretty hard goal to achieve, but I can tell you that it is not impossible. I must admit that it does require a concentrated effort and a lot of work to try to get back some of the little pleasures that we may have enjoyed as children. "Your living is determined not so much by what life brings to you as by the attitude you bring to life; not so much by what happens to you as by the way your mind looks at what happens."[112]

It's neat how much information I actually processed as a child and how much I stored in the recesses of my mind. Parents are very influential in forming the values of their children. Children in their own innocence readily pass along this information. I was somehow or other taught to believe that I was less than some of my friends. This is how I came to describe myself as the underdog. You know the kind that is certainly not voted the most likely to succeed. Yup...that one! I'm referring to the one who has to work a little harder to prove herself. Am I describing someone you might know? By any chance is it you?

Right about now I want to go back to my storytelling ways. I am quite well known for this little habit of mine. If I can tell a story to better explain what I mean, you can be darn sure I will do just that. One of the stories I want to share with you comes from a second grade reader that was used when I taught school so many years ago. It was called **Stone Soup**. The reason this story has come to mind several times over the years is because of a somewhat embarrassing situation that took place in my life. I've already mentioned that after I left teaching, I was employed by a major bank where I was asked to give my opinion on a method of management at a meeting. I was actually stunned to be called upon to put in my two cents worth. I was almost dumbstruck. I was like a deer in the headlights of an oncoming car. Finding myself in this awkward situation was totally new to me and my resources were very limited as far as the business world was concerned.

The first thing that popped into my head came from a second grade reader from my previous teaching experience.

The fact that we were discussing the roles of individuals within the financial institution seemed to give new relevance to this particular story. This was a story or fairytale that took place during extremely difficult times. According to the story, there was so much poverty, very little to eat and a growing desperation by the people. In essence, everyone was pretty well starving to death. There were many small towns scattered about and the towns people were at there wits end in trying to just survive. One day, a stranger came into town and right in the middle of the town square; he proceeded to light a fire. Out of curiosity, several of the local folks gathered around and asked him what he was doing. He decided to tell them that he was making stone soup when in reality he was actually starving just like them. Most of them jeered and laughed at him because they all knew that there was no such thing as stone soup. The stranger insisted that there was indeed a fine recipe and he knew it. After he lit the fire, he continued to stoke it. When it was big and hot enough, he got a large metal container and filled it with water. He put it over the fire and added a few stones to it and watched it start to boil. More and more people gathered to watch this man and observe his foolishness. After the water was boiling at full force he asked the large group that had now gathered, if any one of them happened to have a tasty onion to add to his stone soup recipe. Sure enough one person happened to have his request. He then asked if anyone else happened to have a bone or two that could enhance the taste of his delicious recipe. Sure enough, some one did. Before you know it, they were others who were standing around that had a few other ingredients to add to this stranger's recipe for stone soup. After adding all that the town folks had to offer, he ended up with quite a tasty pot of soup. He then ladled it out for all to enjoy. In the story when this stranger walked into that poverty stricken town, he had nothing to offer except a good idea. Not one of them could make a meal with what each had, but by combining what they had together they could make a delicious soup that could be shared by all.

Therefore, I sat around that corporate table for the very first time in my life and related this story. I explained to them that we all have something to offer but we all need to work together to make the best of it. The employees at the bottom of any pyramidal structure, similar to the employees in the middle or at the top, have something vital to offer in order to enhance the success of the business. I felt that in order to promote the new philosophy that we were discussing at this particular meeting, we would be wise to remember the moral of this particular story. The best recipe to make our business a success was to appreciate the contributions of all levels of workers within the organization. My supervisor, who asked me what I thought in the first place, was impressed enough with my story that at a future meeting in another boardroom at an even higher level up the business ladder, put me on the spot once again. She asked me to repeat that story to this level of management and I did. We tried to make a small difference in the way that people think. I have a sneaking suspicion that we touched a few lives in our own way.

Please...just keep in mind that we all have something to offer in this life of ours. As small as you may think it is, it is very important to add what you have to the recipe of life. Contribute what you can to help others in a positive and productive way and you will enjoy the results of your own efforts. You will get to share in the "soup" at the end of the day because your own personal efforts have been added to the final product. You most definitely do have something to add, you only need to find the courage to do it. You may very well be like the stranger with a good idea. Explore every possibility. You may even surprise yourself! I learned something very important at that first board meeting. You don't need to be a boss/supervisor to be a leader. This was a very important realization to me as my new role in this organization unfolded. I also learned that you can have power without position. "Leadership is action, not position."[113] Think about that one. What kind of power do you have? Is it positive or negative? How do you influence the people in your life? Yes, we all have a role to play in all that we say and do. "I found that I could find the energy…that I could find the determination to keep going. I learned that your mind can amaze your body, if you just keep telling yourself, I can do it…I can do it…I can do it!"[114] You can turn your life around by just looking at yourself and deciding what you have to positively offer in life and then choosing to offer it. You will not only enhance your life, but it will have the domino effect of enhancing the lives of those around you. Use your God given talents in a way that they have never been utilized before. There is not one of us who hasn't been born without at least one talent. You are no exception. Find yours and then start building from there. It's the best way to go. "You have a remarkable ability which you never acknowledged before. It is to look at a situation and know whether you can do it. And I mean really know the answer."[115] How are you going to govern your life? How do you use your influence over others?

"The end of good government is to cultivate humanity, and promote the happiness of all."[116]

CONCLUSION

I want to say at the onset of the conclusion to this book that according to Victor Hugo, "there is one thing stronger than all the armies in the world, and that is an idea whose time has come."[117] I have wanted to use this quote since the writing of my very first book. In fact, it was in the final chapter of that book, but on the recommendation of my editor the whole paragraph that contained it, was deleted. I may not be in the same league as Victor Hugo but it doesn't mean I don't have something important to say. This is the reason that I included it here today because I still believe it as wholeheartedly as I did then. You, too, may have something important to say or do. Things may not fall into place as quickly or as successfully as we might always hope for, but with patience and faith you can count on the fact that they will. "I am convinced that the world is not a mere bog in which men and women trample themselves in the mire and die. Something magnificent is taking place here amid the cruelties and tragedies, and the supreme challenge to intelligence is that of making the noblest and best in our curious heritage prevail."[118]

All of my manuscripts which are faith based are drawn from my own personal inspiration and relationship with God.

I don't know the plan. All I know is that I am, as are you, part of the Divine Plan which is far greater than anyone of us could possibly imagine. If things don't go quite as we see fit, it doesn't mean to say that all won't turn out for the better. Miracles take time. Often times, life can appear magical but miracles don't happen quite as fast or in the same way. We must exercise extreme patience and diligence in order for our own personal plan to unfold. God is not in a hurry. "The sculptor will chip off all unnecessary material to set the angel free. Nature will chip and pound us remorselessly to bring out our possibilities. She will strip us of wealth, humble our pride, humiliate our ambition, let us down from the ladder of fame, will discipline us in a thousand ways, if she can develop a little character. Everything must give way to that. Wealth is nothing, position is nothing, fame is nothing, manhood is everything."[119] Good things can and do happen to good people. God has promised us many things and is true to His word. We must count on that in our daily lives. "Each experience through which we pass operates ultimately for our good….This is a correct attitude to adopt…and we must be able to see it in that light."[120] We don't always recognize the work of God, but if we are patient with ourselves and take the time to reflect, we will create the opportunity to see exactly how God works.

Don't be fooled. This is God's world. He created it out of love just as we are also created out of love. Everything in it belongs to God. Everything will come true just as God has predicted. Each and every one of us means the world to God. Take the time to draw from the Divine Energy that lives within and you will see clearer. Trust in God and the plan laid out for you. God will not let you down. Also trust that God knows exactly what He is doing and you will not be disappointed. Stop, look, listen to all that is being taught to you. Faith in a loving God will help restore your faith in yourself. Love others as God has loved you and you will give a human face to God in the world around you. Trust in God more than you have ever trusted before and you will have the courage to face life in a way that you never dreamed possible. The gifts of faith…love…trust…give new hope for us all and are a rewarding and gratifying motto to live by. Try to bear in mind, that God has given us extraordinary powers. "Deep within man dwell those slumbering powers; powers that would astonish him, that he never dreamed of possessing; forces that would revolutionize his life if aroused and put into action."[121] Also, try to remember that God has appointed us as guardians of this world. He has given us the honor of being co-creators will all the responsibility that goes with it. It would seem that at times, God has shown more faith in us as humankind than we actually have shown in God. Think…reflect…decide. Yes, we all have freedom of choice. "We must determine whether we really want freedom--whether we are willing to dare the perils of… rebirth…For we never take a step forward without surrendering something that we may have held dear, without dying to that which has been."[122] Yes…think….reflect, and then decide! There is only one right way to go and that is "Up"!

BONUS CHAPTER

Growing Up and Liking It

Hiss...My Name is Gossip

I already know that this is not going to be an easy chapter to write; however, I also know that it begs to be written. Do any of you have a pet peeve of one kind or another? Well, I have to admit that I do. I know that I have more than one, but one of my biggest pet peeves is the act of gossiping and the damage it does. This is one of those subjects, that no matter how hard I am going to try, it will be very hard to flower up.

The first thing I need to do is remind everyone of the power of communication. I know that in my last book I wrote about it quite extensively, but I only want to touch base on it by telling you a couple of short stories in this book. Many years ago, I took a class on effective communication. During that class, the professor wanted to demonstrate to the students just how much our words can change as they are repeated from one person to the other. He proceeded to get about ten people to go up to the front of the class. He then whispered a sentence into the ear of the first student in the line. After this, he instructed the student to whisper the sentence to the next student in line. Each person was to continue this process until the sentence got to the last person down the line. Subsequently, the professor asked the first person to repeat the sentence he or she had heard at the beginning of this procedure. Then the last student was asked to do the same thing. I cannot tell you how different the sentence was when comparing what the first student said to what the last one did. Words got changed all the way down the line.

The second little story I am going to tell you is a true story as well. One day my husband was golfing with his lifelong friend. Over the years we had also become friends with his wife, and we got together many times as couples. On one particular day, this man told my husband that his wife's elderly father had suffered a heart attack. When my husband got home from his golf game he proceeded to tell me that our friend's father-in-law had passed away. Due to the fact that we had known this couple almost our entire lives, we knew each other's family quite well. Therefore, I then passed this information along to some members of my own family. It was then decided that we should send some flowers to express our condolences and show our respect. My husband and I happened to be visiting with this couple a day or two afterwards, so we opted to just deliver the flowers ourselves. You cannot imagine the expression on our friend's face when we arrived at the door with our gift and offered our sympathy on her father's death. Her father did have a heart attack, but he had not passed away. Somehow or other, my husband assumed that he had when he was told about it. When I received the information, I acted on it. Thank goodness these people were such good friends and no feelings were hurt. As red faced as we may have been, they were pretty amused by our blunder. A month or so later, her father actually did pass away, and they reminded us of the fact that we had already respectfully acknowledged his passing. This second story demonstrates that even as good as our intentions may be, we can still goof up and incorrectly repeat some information we have heard.

Now, I am going to get into the less desirable part of this chapter. News, whether it is good, sad, or bad can go into what I refer to as another zone. There is nothing wrong with repeating information that needs to be repeated. Usually it is totally appropriate to share information because this is how we communicate with each other. It's what we share, how we share it, and why we share it that makes all the difference between whether it is appropriate or not. This is the part I find most difficult to write because it is about a subject I find so negative and ugly. It's the subject of gossip. Gossip is very different from sharing news. Sometimes I think we all know the difference, and then when I observe some of the damage that gossip can do, I'm not so sure. Most gossipers pride themselves on being well intentioned when they repeat something they actually know they shouldn't. Others don't care. Gossip has the tendency to be more than the mere sharing of any kind of news because it involves a lot more extrapolation about the news itself by the person or persons passing it along. The gossipy one has the desire to give a lot of his/her personal opinions rather than just the facts.

It is very easy to fall into this trap. Subsequently, the person receiving this information may pass it along the same way or further add his/her opinions to it. Remember those ten students at the front of the class? Well, the misinterpretation or misrepresentation of what may or may not be going on in another person's life is what starts the rumors. It's what gets the gossip mill going in the first place. We all have the tendency, at one time or another, to be the receiver of gossip or the repeater of it. No one, no matter how good his/her intentions may very well be, has been exempt from gossip of one form or another at some point in life. There is no use pussyfooting around this topic. Gossip is a fact of life! A good rule of thumb to use before we repeat what we have heard is to ask ourselves if it is really necessary to do so. If the answer is *"no,"* then we must ask ourselves why we would repeat what we have heard and would we want it said about ourselves.

I have had the habit of cutting out many articles of interest over the years. This one is from a local newspaper. The message was of great interest to me then and still is to this day. I can't even say which local newspaper featured it, because one of our two main papers stopped publishing some time during the period I started to collect these articles, which was well over twenty-five years ago. The article itself is called "Nobody's Friend." In it, gossip is named as nobody's friend. It states that gossip has, "no respect for justice."[123] It goes on to say that it can "maim without killing, break hearts and ruin lives."[124] It indicates that the more gossip is repeated, the more it is apt to be believed. The unknown writer of the article says that the victims of the effects of gossip are powerless. It is almost as if, the more a victim tries to stop a rumor, the more impetus the rumor has. According to this article, gossip can "tarnish a reputation, wreck marriages, ruin careers, and cause sleepless nights, heartache and indigestion."[125] I cannot come up with any better words to describe what the author of this article had to say as far as the damage that gossip can do or the pain that it can cause. It can "make innocent people cry in their pillows."[126]

As far as I'm concerned, gossip can never be good. The unknown author of this article further proves this point by saying that gossip hisses just like its name. It includes all types of gossip; whether it is office gossip, shop gossip, party gossip, or telephone gossip. The article specifically states that "before you repeat a story, ask yourself, is it true? Is it harmless? Is it necessary? If it isn't, don't repeat it."[127] As far as I'm concerned, this is darn good advice. As difficult as I know it is to follow, making the effort to do so is all anyone can ask. People think that swords can hurt people and cause bodily damage. Yes they can, but words can be like swords that cut even deeper, so deep that some may never heal. I can't stress this enough! I found another little quote, which coincides with the previous mentioned article. In it, Tryon Edwards states, "To murder a character is as truly a crime as to murder the body."[128] He obviously feels as strongly as I do about the subject because in another quote he goes on to say, "The tongue of the slanderer is brother to the dagger of the assassin."[129]

I think I've made my opinion on this subject pretty clear. It's one of those topics that I felt really needed to be addressed. Due to the fact that gossip is so averse to me, I want to make this chapter as short and precise as possible. Remember, the key to stopping gossip is to know the difference between sharing news and sharing gossip. Once you figure this out and make a concerted effort to stop gossip, a lot less damage will be done. It has been my experience that if you refuse to gossip, eventually people will stop sharing gossip with you. This habit makes for cleaner living. You may not know everything that is going on, but ask yourself, do you really need to?

Step 4 ~ Gossip is never good no matter how you look at it! I'm suggesting a few more questions to further ask yourself. By doing so, you may get a better understanding of the negative consequences of gossiping and how you can avoid it. Have you ever repeated information you know you shouldn't? How did it make you feel? Make sure to surround yourself with people who genuinely care and love you and your friends. This is a great way to keep away from gossiping!

TO CONTACT AUTHOR:

WEBSITE

http://www.doloresayotte.com

BLOG SITE

http://www.doloresayotte.wordpress.com

BIBLIOGRAPHY

"John Ruskin quotes." BrainyQuote.
http://www.brainyquote.com/quotes/authors/j/john_ruskin_5.html
(Accessed May 11, 2009).

"Theodore Parker quotes." Diversions Page, Winnipeg Free Press, Wednesday, June 10, 2009.

Wynn Davis, The Best of Success (Lombard, Illinois: Successories Publishing, 1992).
"Elizabeth Stuart Phelps quotes." Thinkexist.com,
http://thinkexist.com/quotation/it_is_not_the_straining_for_great_things_that_is/322794.html (Accessed May 11, 2009).

"Napoleon Hill quotes," BrainyQuote,
http://www.brainyquote.com/quotes/authors/n/napoleon_hill_3.html. (Accessed May 11, 2009).

"Orison Swett Marden quotes," Noyemi Famous Quotes,
http://www.noyemi.com/quote128888.html. (Accessed May 11, 2009).

"Lao-Tse quotes." BrainyQuote,
http://www.brainyquote.com/quotes/keywords/difficult.html (Accessed May 11, 2009).

"Tyron Edwards quotes." The Quotations Page.
http://www.quotationspage.com/quote/2712.html (Accessed May 11, 2009).

"Albert Schweitzer quotes." Thinkexist.com,
http://thinkexist.com/quotation/i_know_of_no_great_men_except_those_who_have/145878.html (Accessed May 11, 2009).

"Eleanor Roosevelt quotes." BrainyQuote.
http://www.brainyquote.com/quotes/authors/e/eleanor_roosevelt_3.html (Accessed May 11, 2009).

"Ira Progoff quotes." Sy Safransky, Sunbeams A Book of Quotations (Berkeley, California: North Atlantic Books, 1990).

"Mike Singletary quotes." Thinkexist.com.
http://thinkexist.com/quotes/mike_singletary/ (Accessed May 11, 2009).

"Publilius Syrus quotes." BrainyQuote.
http://www.brainyquote.com/quotes/authors/p/publilius_syrus_2.html (Accessed May 11, 2009).

"Sanskrit Proverb quotes." Diversions Page, Winnipeg Free Press, Wednesday, April 29, 2009.

"Albert Einstein quotes." Thinkexist.com.
http://thinkexist.com/quotation/life_is_like_riding_a_bicycle-to_keep_your/327432.html (Accessed May 11, 2009).

"Dale Carnegie quotes." Diversions Page. Winnipeg Free Press, Tuesday, May 12, 2009.

"William Arthur Ward quotes," Thinkexist.com.
http://thinkexist.com/quotation/the_pessimist_complains_about_the_wind-the/227505.html (Accessed May 11, 2009).

"Regina Brett quotes." Bob Rodkin, The Good News Blog, June 5, 2009.
http://bobrodkin.blogspot.com/2009/06/45-lessons-life-taught-me-regina-brett.html (Accessed June 15, 2009).

"Helen Keller quotes." Diversions Page, Winnipeg Free Press, Sunday, May 10, 2009.

"Maya Angelou quotes." The Quotations Page.
http://www.quotationspage.com/quote/31264.html (Accessed May 11, 2009).

"Benjamin Disraeli quotes." BrainyQuote.
http://www.brainyquote.com/quotes/authors/b/benjamin_disraeli_6.html (Accessed May 5, 2009).

"Milton Berle quotes." Thinkexist.com.
http://thinkexist.com/quotation/if_opportunity_doesn-t_knock-build_a_door/214986.html (Accessed May 11, 2009).

"Jim Ryun quotes." The Quote Garden.
http://www.quotegarden.com/habits.html (Accessed May 11, 2009).

"Dale Carnegie quotes." QuotationsBook. http://quotationsbook.com/quote/26691/ (Accessed May 11, 2009).

"Henry Ford quotes." Quotation. http://www.quotatio.com/f/ford-henry-failure-is-the-opportunity-to-begin-060755.html (Accessed May 11, 2009).

"Samuel Johnson quotes," Diversions Page, Winnipeg Free Press, Thursday, July 9, 2009.

"F. Scott Fitzgerald quotes." Thinkexist.com. http://thinkexist.com/quotes/f._scott_fitzgerald/ (Accessed June 15, 2009).

"Alexander Woolcott quotes." BrainyQuote. http://www.brainyquote.com/quotes/authors/a/alexander_woollcott.html (Accessed June 15, 2009).

"Fulton Sheen quotes." Thinkexist.com. http://thinkexist.com/quotes/fulton_j._sheen/ (Accessed June 15, 2009).

"William James quotes." The Quotations Page. http://www.quotationspage.com/quotes/William_James/ (Accessed June 15, 2009).

"John W. Gardner quotes." CreatingMinds.org. http://creatingminds.org/quotes/problems.htm (Accessed June 15, 2009).

"Claude M. Bristol quotes." About.com. http://quotations.about.com/od/stillmorefamouspeople/a/ClaudeMBristol1.htm (Accessed June 15, 2009).

"Thomas Paine quotes." BrainyQuote. http://www.brainyquote.com/quotes/authors/t/thomas_paine_3.html (Accessed June 15, 2009).

From the song These Boots Are Made for Walkin, Reprise Records. Lyrics by Lee Hazelwood, 1966.

"Albert Einstein quotes." Buzzle.com. http://www.buzzle.com/articles/famous-wisdom-quotes.html (Accessed June 15, 2009).

"Mother Teresa quotes." QuoteDB. http://www.quotedb.com/quotes/1932 (Accessed June 15, 2009).

"Mahatma Ghandi quotes." Thinkexist.com. http://thinkexist.com/quotation/the-future-depends-on-what-we-do-in-the-present/748149.html (Accessed June 15, 2009).

"Albert Einstein quotes." BrainyQuote. http://www.brainyquote.com/quotes/authors/a/albert_einstein_8.html (Accessed June 15, 2009).

"American Proverb quotes." Best Web Quotes. http://www.bestwebquotes.com/quote/16538-kindness-is-the-noblest-weapon-to-conquer-with.html (Accessed June 15, 2009).

"Oprah Winfrey quotes." Joy of Quotes.com. http://www.joyofquotes.com/happiness_quotes.html (Accessed June 15, 2009).

"Arnay Jones quotes." WorldofQuotes.com. http://www.worldofquotes.com/author/Janos-Arnay/1/index.html (Accessed June 15, 2009).

"Winston Churchill quotes." BrainyQuote. http://www.brainyquote.com/quotes/authors/w/winston_churchill.html (Accessed June 15, 2009).

"Ronald Reagan quotes." The Quotations Page. http://www.quotationspage.com/quote/33740.html (Accessed June 15, 2009).

"James T. McCay quotes." QuotationsBook. http://quotationsbook.com/author/4844/ (Accessed June 15, 2009).

"Theodore Roosevelt quotes." BrainyQuote. http://www.brainyquote.com/quotes/quotes/t/theodorero120667.html (Accessed June 15, 2009).

"Vincent Van Gogh quotes," BrainyQuote, http://www.brainyquote.com/quotes/authors/v/vincent_van_gogh.html (Accessed June 16, 2009).

"Mary Pickford quotes." Diversions Page, Winnipeg Free Press, Thursday, May 13, 2009.

"Zig Zigler quotes." BeatInspirationalQuotes4u.com. http://www.bestinspirationalquotes4u.com/Success/Learningfrfailure/learningfrfailure.html (Accessed June 16, 2009).

"Author Unknown." Flickr. http://www.flickr.com/photos/scottishswan/3358509432/ (Accessed June 16, 2009).

"William Feather quotes." BrainyQuote. http://www.brainyquote.com/quotes/authors/w/william_feather_2.html (Accessed June 16, 2009).

"Joshua J. Marine quotes." Thinkexist.com. http://thinkexist.com/quotation/challenges_are_what_make_life_interesting/209814.html (Accessed June 16, 2009).

"Eleanor Roosevelt quotes." BrainyQuote. http://www.brainyquote.com/quotes/authors/e/eleanor_roosevelt_4.html (Accessed June 16, 2009).

"Willa Foster quotes." WorldofQuotes.com. http://www.worldofquotes.com/author/Willa-A-Foster/1/index.html (Accessed June 16, 2009).

"Abraham Lincoln quotes." BrainyQuote. http://www.brainyquote.com/quotes/authors/a/abraham_lincoln_5.html (Accessed June 16, 2009).

"Vince Lombardi quotes." QuoteDB. http://www.quotedb.com/quotes/2420 (Accessed June 16, 2009).

"Roy Moody quotes." QuotesandPoems.com. http://www.quotesandpoem.com/quotes/listquotes/author/roy-e.-moody (Accessed June 16, 2009).

"Vernon Law quotes." BrainyQuote. http://www.brainyquote.com/quotes/authors/v/vernon_law.html (Accessed June 16, 2009).

"Aesop's Fables quotes." 2009 Wisconsin Evangelical Lutheran Synod. http://www.wels.net/cgi-bin/site.pl?1518&cuTopic_topicID=47&cuItem_itemID=19581 (Accessed June 16, 2009).

"Ralph Waldo Emerson quotes." BrainyQuote. http://www.brainyquote.com/quotes/authors/r/ralph_waldo_emerson_9.html (Accessed June 16, 2009).

"Michael Korda quotes." Thinkexist.com. http://thinkexist.com/quotes/michael_korda/2.html (Accessed June 16, 2009).

"Louis L. Mann quotes." WorldofQuotes.com. http://www.worldofquotes.com/author/Louis-L.-Mann/1/index.html (Accessed June 16, 2009).

"Franklin Roosevelt quotes." The Quotations Page. http://www.quotationspage.com/quotes/Franklin_D._Roosevelt (Accessed May 5, 2009).

"William Arthur Ward quotes." Thinkexist.com. http://thinkexist.com/quotes/william_arthur_ward/ (Accessed June 17, 2009).

"John Wise quotes." Diversions Page, Winnipeg Free Press, Thursday, June 7, 2009.

"Victor Hugo quotes." BrainyQuote. http://www.brainyquote.com/quotes/authors/v/victor_hugo_8.html (Accessed June 17, 2009).

ENDNOTES

[1] "John Ruskin quotes," BrainyQuote, http://www.brainyquote.com/quotes/authors/j/john_ruskin_5.html.
[2] "Theodore Parker quotes," Diversions Page, Winnipeg Free Press, Wednesday, June 10, 2009.
[3] "Samuel Smiles quotes," Wynn Davis, The Best of Success (Lombard, Illinois, Successories Publishing, 1992), P.332.
[4] "Elizabeth Stuart Phelps quotes," Thinkexist.com, http://thinkexist.com/quotation/it_is_not_the_straining_for_great_things_that_is/322794.html.
[5] "Albert Low quotes," Wynn Davis, The Best of Success (Lombard, Illinois, Successories Publishing, 1992), P.51.
[6] "Vernon Howard quotes," Ibid, P.51.
[7] "Michel Eyquem De Montaigne quotes," Ibid, P.77.
[8] "Adlai Stevenson quotes," Ibid, P.320.
[9] "Soren Kierkegard quotes," Ibid, P.320.
[10] "Carl Frederick quotes," Ibid, P.24.
[11] "Joseph Sugarman quotes," Ibid, P.227.
[12] "Napoleon Hill quotes," BrainyQuote, http://www.brainyquote.com/quotes/authors/n/napoleon_hill_3.html.
[13] "Orison Swett Marden quotes," Noyemi Famous Quotes, http://www.noyemi.com/quote128888.html.
[14] "Vincent Van Gogh quotes," BrainyQuote, http://www.brainyquote.com/quotes/authors/v/vincent_van_gogh.html.
[15] "David Viscott quotes," Wynn Davis, The Best of Success (Lombard, Illinois, Successories Publishing, 1992), P.112.
[16] "Dan Dierdorf quotes," Ibid, P.155.
[17] "H. Stanley Judd quotes," Ibid, P.156.
[18] "Ben Stein quotes," Ibid, P.152.
[19] "Mary Pickford quotes," Diversions Page, Winnipeg Free Press, Thursday, May 13, 2009.
[20] "Zig Zigler quotes," BeatInspirationalQuotes4u.com, http://www.bestinspirationalquotes4u.com/Success/Learningfrfailure/learningfrfailure.html.
[21] "Author Unknown," Flickr, http://www.flickr.com/photos/scottishswan/3358509432/.
[22] "William Feather quotes." BrainyQuote, http://www.brainyquote.com/quotes/authors/w/william_feather_2.html.

[23] "Joshua J. Marine quotes," Thinkexist.com, http://thinkexist.com/quotation/challenges_are_what_make_life_interesting/209814.html.
[24] "Eleanor Roosevelt quotes," BrainyQuote, http://www.brainyquote.com/quotes/authors/e/eleanor_roosevelt_4.html.
[25] "Willa Foster quotes," WorldofQuotes.com, http://www.worldofquotes.com/author/Willa-A-Foster/1/index.html.
[26] "Abraham Lincoln quotes," BrainyQuote, http://www.brainyquote.com/quotes/authors/a/abraham_lincoln_5.html.
[27] "Vince Lombardi quotes," QuoteDB, http://www.quotedb.com/quotes/2420.
[28] "Roy Moody quotes," QuotesandPoems.com, http://www.quotesandpoem.com/quotes/listquotes/author/roy-e.-moody.
[29] "Vernon Law quotes," BrainyQuote, http://www.brainyquote.com/quotes/authors/v/vernon_law.html.
[30] "Aesop's Fables quotes," 2009 Wisconsin Evangelical Lutheran Synod, http://www.wels.net/cgi-bin/site.pl?1518&cuTopic_topicID=47&cuItem_itemID=19581.
[31] "Ralph Waldo Emerson quotes," BrainyQuote, http://www.brainyquote.com/quotes/authors/r/ralph_waldo_emerson_9.html.
[32] "Michael Korda quotes," Thinkexist.com, http://thinkexist.com/quotes/michael_korda/2.html.
[33] "Regina Brett quotes," Bob Rodkin, The Good News Blog, Posted June 5, 2009, http://bobrodkin.blogspot.com/2009/06/45-lessons-life-taught-me-regina-brett.html.
[34] "Louis L. Mann quotes," WorldofQuotes.com, http://www.worldofquotes.com/author/Louis-L.-Mann/1/index.html.
[35] "Franklin Roosevelt quotes," The Quotations Page, http://www.quotationspage.com/quotes/Franklin_D._Roosevelt.
[36] "Henry Ford quotes," Wynn Davis, The Best of Success (Lombard, Illinois, Successories Publishing, 1992), P164.
[37] "Lao-Tse quotes," BrainyQuote, http://www.brainyquote.com/quotes/keywords/difficult.html.
[38] "Napoleon Hill quotes," Wynn Davis, The Best of Success (Lombard, Illinois, Successories Publishing, 1992), P.226.
[39] "Michael Korda quotes," Ibid, P.274.
[40] "Orison Swett Marden quotes," Ibid, P.225.
[41] "Orison Swett Marden quotes," Ibid, P.225.
[42] "James Allen quotes," Ibid, P.24.
[43] "W. Clement Stone quotes," Ibid, P.24.
[44] "Thomas Merton quotes," Ibid, P.273.

[45] "Albert Schweitzer quotes," Ibid, P.283.
[46] "B.C. Forbes quotes," Ibid, P.283.
[47] "Tyron Edwards quotes," The Quotations Page, http://www.quotationspage.com/quote/2712.html.
[48] "Isaac Bashevis Singer quotes," Wynn Davis, The Best of Success (Lombard, Illinois, Successories Publishing, 1992), P.255.
[49] "Robert Collier quotes," Ibid, P.323.
[50] "Maxwell Maltz quotes," Ibid, P.256.
[51] "Orison Swett Marden quotes," Ibid, P.284.
[52] "W. Clement Stone quotes," Ibid, P.24.
[53] "Albert Schweitzer quotes," Thinkexist.com, http://thinkexist.com/quotation/i_know_of_no_great_men_except_those_who_have/145878.html.
[54] "Voltaire quotes," Wynn Davis, The Best of Success (Lombard, Illinois, Successories Publishing, 1992), P.282.
[55] "Eleanor Roosevelt quotes," BrainyQuote, http://www.brainyquote.com/quotes/authors/e/eleanor_roosevelt_3.html.
[56] "Ira Progoff quotes," Sy Safransky, Sunbeams A Book of Quotations (Berkeley, California, North Atlantic Books, 1990), P.56.
[57] "Mike Singletary quotes," Thinkexist.com, http://thinkexist.com/quotes/mike_singletary/.
[58] "Publilius Syrus quotes," BrainyQuote, http://www.brainyquote.com/quotes/authors/p/publilius_syrus_2.html.
[59] "Sanskrit Proverb quotes," Diversions Page, Winnipeg Free Press, Wednesday, April 29, 2009.
[60] "Albert Einstein quotes," Thinkexist.com, http://thinkexist.com/quotation/life_is_like_riding_a_bicycle-to_keep_your/327432.html.
[61] "Dale Carnegie quotes," Diversions Page, Winnipeg Free Press, Tuesday, May 12, 2009.
[62] "William Arthur Ward quotes," Thinkexist.com, http://thinkexist.com/quotation/the_pessimist_complains_about_the_wind-the/227505.html.
[63] "Regina Brett quotes," Bob Rodkin, The Good News Blog, June 5, 2009, http://bobrodkin.blogspot.com/2009/06/45-lessons-life-taught-me-regina-brett.html.
[64] "Helen Keller quotes," Diversions Page, Winnipeg Free Press, Sunday, May 10, 2009.
[65] "Regina Brett quotes," Bob Rodkin, The Good News Blog, June 5, 2009, http://bobrodkin.blogspot.com/2009/06/45-lessons-life-taught-me-regina-brett.html.
[66] Ibid.

[67] Ibid.
[68] "Maya Angelou quotes," The Quotations Page, http://www.quotationspage.com/quote/31264.html.
[69] "Benjamin Disraeli quotes," BrainyQuote, http://www.brainyquote.com/quotes/authors/b/benjamin_disraeli_6.html.
[70] "Milton Berle quotes," Thinkexist.com, http://thinkexist.com/quotation/if_opportunity_doesn-t_knock-build_a_door/214986.html.
[71] "Jim Ryun quotes," The Quote Garden, http://www.quotegarden.com/habits.html.
[72] "Dale Carnegie quotes," QuotationsBook, http://quotationsbook.com/quote/26691/.
[73] "Henry Ford quotes," Quotatio, http://www.quotatio.com/f/ford-henry-failure-is-the-opportunity-to-begin-060755.html.
[74] "Maxwell Maltz quotes," Wynn Davis, The Best of Success (Lombard, Illinois, Successories Publishing, 1992), P.174.
[75] "Joseph Sugarman quotes," Ibid, P.179.
[76] "Samuel Johnson quotes," Diversions Page, Winnipeg Free Press, Thursday, July 9, 2009.
[77] "Orison Swett Marden quotes," Wynn Davis, The Best of Success (Lombard, Illinois, Successories Publishing, 1992), P.168.
[78] "Jo Coudert quotes," Ibid, P.168.
[79] "Gerald Waterhouse quotes," Ibid, P.180.
[80] "John Stuart Mill quotes," Ibid, P.23.
[81] "Lowell Thomas quotes," Ibid, P.102.
[82] "Wilfred A. Peterson quotes," Ibid, P.103.
[83] "James Allen quotes," Ibid, P184.
[84] "F. Scott Fitzgerald quotes," Thinkexist.com, http://thinkexist.com/quotes/f._scott_fitzgerald/.
[85] "Alexander Woolcott quotes," BrainyQuote, http://www.brainyquote.com/quotes/authors/a/alexander_woollcott.html.
[86] "Fulton Sheen quotes," Thinkexist.com, http://thinkexist.com/quotes/fulton_j._sheen/.
[87] "William James quotes," The Quotations Page, http://www.quotationspage.com/quotes/William_James/.
[88] "John W. Gardner quotes," CreatingMinds.org, http://creatingminds.org/quotes/problems.htm.
[89] "Claude M. Bristol quotes," About.com, http://quotations.about.com/od/stillmorefamouspeople/a/ClaudeMBristol1.htm.
[90] "Thomas Paine quotes," BrainyQuote, http://www.brainyquote.com/quotes/authors/t/thomas_paine_3.html.

[91] From the song These Boots Are Made for Walkin, Reprise Records, Lyrics by Lee Hazelwood, 1966.
[92] "Albert Einstein quotes," Buzzle.com, http://www.buzzle.com/articles/famous-wisdom-quotes.html.
[93] "Mother Teresa quotes," QuoteDB, http://www.quotedb.com/quotes/1932.
[94] From the song These Boots Are Made for Walkin, Reprise Records, Lyrics by Lee Hazelwood, 1966.
[95] "Regina Brett quotes," Bob Rodkin, The Good News Blog, Posted June 5, 2009, http://bobrodkin.blogspot.com/2009/06/45-lessons-life-taught-me-regina-brett.html.
[96] "Mahatma Ghandi quotes," Thinkexist.com, http://thinkexist.com/quotation/the-future-depends-on-what-we-do-in-the-present/748149.html.
[97] "Albert Einstein quotes," BrainyQuote, http://www.brainyquote.com/quotes/authors/a/albert_einstein_8.html.
[98] "American Proverb quotes," Best Web Quotes, http://www.bestwebquotes.com/quote/16538-kindness-is-the-noblest-weapon-to-conquer-with.html.
[99] "Oprah Winfrey quotes," Joy of Quotes.com, http://www.joyofquotes.com/happiness_quotes.html.
[100] "Arnay Jones quotes," WorldofQuotes.com, http://www.worldofquotes.com/author/Janos-Arnay/1/index.html.
[101] "Winston Churchill quotes," BrainyQuote, http://www.brainyquote.com/quotes/authors/w/winston_churchill.html.
[102] "Ronald Reagan quotes," The Quotations Page, http://www.quotationspage.com/quote/33740.html.
[103] "Regina Brett quotes," Bob Rodkin, The Good News Blog, Posted June 5, 2009, http://bobrodkin.blogspot.com/2009/06/45-lessons-life-taught-me-regina-brett.html.
[104] Ibid.
[105] Ibid.
[106] "James T. McCay quotes," QuotationsBook, http://quotationsbook.com/author/4844/.
[107] "Carl Fredericks quotes," Wynn Davis, The Best of Success (Lombard, Illinois, Successories Publishing, 1992), P.254.
[108] "Paul G. Thomas quotes." Ibid, P.23.
[109] "Vernon Howard quotes." Ibid, P.23.
[110] "Theodore Roosevelt quotes," BrainyQuote, http://www.brainyquote.com/quotes/quotes/t/theodorero120667.html.
[111] "William Arthur Ward quotes," Thinkexist.com, http://thinkexist.com/quotes/william_arthur_ward/.

[112] "John Homer Miller quotes," Wynn Davis, The Best of Success (Lombard, Illinois, Successories Publishing, 1992), P.8.
[113] "Donald H. McGannon quotes," Ibid, P.282.
[114] "Jon Erickson quotes," Ibid, P.17.
[115] "Carl Frederick quotes," Ibid, P.17.
[116] "John Wise quotes," Diversions Page, Winnipeg Free Press, Thursday, June 7, 2009.
[117] "Victor Hugo quotes," BrainyQuote, http://www.brainyquote.com/quotes/authors/v/victor_hugo_8.html.
[118] "Charles A. Beard quotes," Wynn Davis, The Best of Success (Lombard, Illinois, Successories Publishing, 1992), P.165.
[119] "Orison Swett Marden quotes," Ibid, P.165.
[120] "Raymond Holliwell quotes," Ibid, P.165.
[121] "Orison Swett Marden quotes," Ibid, P254.
[122] "Virginia Hanson quotes," Ibid, P.133.
[123] "Author Unknown, " BellaOnline: The Voice of Women, http://www.bellaonline.com/articles/art41795.asp.
[124] Ibid.
[125] Ibid.
[126] Ibid.
[127] Ibid.
[128] "Tyron Edwards quotes," Thinkexist.com, http://thinkexist.com/quotes/with/keyword/dagger/.
[129] Ibid.

www.ingramcontent.com/pod-product-compliance
Lightning Source LLC
Chambersburg PA
CBHW071510040426
42444CB00008B/1579